NUMBER TWENTY-FOUR
The Walter Prescott Webb Memorial Lectures

Essays on
Sport History and Sport Mythology

[THE WALTER PRESCOTT WEBB MEMORIAL LECTURES]

Essays on
Sport History
and Sport Mythology

BY ALLEN GUTTMANN, RICHARD D.
MANDELL, STEVEN A. RIESS, STEPHEN
HARDY, AND DONALD G. KYLE

Introduction by JACK W. BERRYMAN
Edited by DONALD G. KYLE
and GARY D. STARK

Published for the University of Texas at Arlington by
Texas A&M University Press : *College Station*

The paper used in this book meets the minimum requirements of the American National Standard for Permanence of Paper for Printed Library Materials,
z39.48-1984. Binding materials have been chosen for durability

∞

Library of Congress Cataloging-in-Publication Data

Essays on sport history and sport mythology / by Allen Guttmann . . .
[et al.] ; introd. by Jack W. Berryman ; edited by Donald G. Kyle and
Gary D. Stark. — 1st ed.
   p.   cm. — (The Walter Prescott Webb memorial lectures ; 24)
   Includes bibliographical references and index.
   ISBN 0-89096-454-8 (alk. paper)
   1. Sports—History.   2. Sports—Social aspects—History.
I. Guttmann, Allen.   II. Kyle, Donald G.   III. Stark, Gary D.,
1948– .   IV. Series.
GV571.E85   1990
796'.09—dc20
                                         90-36414
                                               CIP

Contents

Acknowledgments

THIS VOLUME stems from the twenty-fourth annual Walter Prescott Webb Memorial Lectures held at the University of Texas at Arlington on March 16, 1989. Lectures focusing on the theme of "Sport History and Sport Mythology" were presented by Allen Guttmann, Richard D. Mandell, Stephen Hardy, and Donald G. Kyle. An additional paper by Steven A. Riess was the winning entry in the 1989 Webb-Smith Essay Competition. Revised and edited to varying degrees by the authors and co-editors, the five papers are collected in this volume, with an introduction by Jack W. Berryman. The co-editors wish to thank all the authors for their contributions and their cooperation.

On behalf of the UTA history department, the co-editors would like to acknowledge several benefactors of the Webb lectures. C. B. Smith, Sr., an Austin businessman and former student of Walter Prescott Webb, generously established the Webb Endowment Fund and made possible the publication of the lectures. Jenkins and Virginia Garrett of Fort Worth have long shown both loyalty and generosity to UTA. Recently the Webb lecture series has received major support from the Rudolf Hermanns' Endowment for the Liberal Arts. Dr. Wendell Nedderman, president of UTA, has been instrumental in obtaining such funding for the series. We would also like to acknowledge the assistance of Kenneth Philp, chairman of the history department, and Stephen Maizlish, chairman of the Webb lectures committee.

Finally, this year's volume is dedicated to Sandra L. Myres, professor of history at UTA. For years, as a pioneer and mentor of the series, Dr. Myres has selflessly contributed her energy and scholarly expertise to the Webb lectures. That the series continues to be an academic success story is largely due to the example she has set.

DONALD G. KYLE
GARY D. STARK

Essays on
Sport History and Sport Mythology

JACK W. BERRYMAN

Introduction

As a universal but culturally varied human activity, sport has always been a fascinating topic, but recently sport historians have been studying the phenomenon in more serious and sophisticated ways. We are becoming increasingly aware that sport history invites sport mythologizing, a tendency to misinterpret, oversimplify, misrepresent, or even falsify the actual record. Accordingly, the essays in this volume examine the overlap and the interaction between sport history and sport mythology. As president of the North American Society for Sport History and former editor of the *Journal of Sport History*, it pleases me to see the department of history at the University of Texas at Arlington and Texas A&M University Press honoring the late Professor Webb by publishing these five sport history essays.

That sport history was chosen as a suitable topic for the Webb lectures is indicative of the recent stature and acceptance of the subject in academic circles. Once believed to be the domain of collectors, trivia buffs, and antiquarians, sport history as a significant and legitimate field of scholarly endeavor has come into its own over the past fifteen years. This is evidenced by books published by notable presses, professional historical societies devoted to the subject, sessions at national and international conferences, journals specializing in sport history, and sport history topics appearing in respected professional journals. These developments and more were highlighted in a special issue of the *Journal of Sport History* in 1983 that was devoted to "The Promise of Sport History: Progress and Prospects." Since then, sport history as a field has continued to prosper and become even more firmly situated within the academic community.

As Donald G. Kyle says in the introduction to his essay, sport history, like all disciplines when they mature, is entering a revisionistic and demythologizing stage. "Many popular beliefs and traditional scholarly interpretations concerning sport in various ages and cultures are being reevaluated and modified." Modern sport historians are not only discovering new "facts" and rejecting old myths; they are broadening their conceptual horizons and investigating the origins and operations of sport mythology.

The authors of these five essays are fine representatives of the new scholarship in sport history. Each has published extensively and has been associated with the field for a number of years. Their current work is indicative of what is happening within this exciting subdiscipline of history and sport studies.

These essays are not simply rejections of specific falsehoods or tall tales about sport. Rather each essay, in some distinctive manner, confronts the problem of general preconceptions and misconceptions in the study of sport history. The authors ask fundamental questions: what is sport, what is its significance over time, and how can sport be studied effectively? They also grapple with issues of change and continuity in sport, ideological influences, and historical relativism in the practice and study of sport.

Donald G. Kyle, one of the organizers of these Webb Lectures, illustrates through his own work on ancient sport history that the field is moving into the revisionistic stage. He analyzes myths about Greek sport as evidenced in the writings of the influential classicist and historian of ancient sport, E. Norman Gardiner. Gardiner popularized the myth of the decline of ancient Greek sport; he saw Greek sport reaching its height in the form of amateur Panhellenic games, but soon thereafter falling victim to its own popularity and being brought down by excessive honors for victors, over-competition, over-specialization, and professionalism. Kyle challenges this scenario but, more importantly, he examines Gardiner's life and ideas to demonstrate sport history's potential for misinterpretation on the level of what he calls "macro-mythology." He concludes that given Gardiner's "personal involvement in sport, teaching, and classical studies, and given the athleticism, amateurism, and Hellenism of the era, it was perhaps inevitable that Gardiner share and perpetuate myths about ancient sport."

Stephen Hardy launches a broad study of the issue of change or continuity in sport and the conceptualization of the essence of sport in ancient versus modern societies. He tends to disagree with the work of Guttmann, Mandell, and Adelman, who represent the "modernist" school, which sees sport as we know it as distinctively modern and different from the sport of pre-modern cultures; and he sides more with the recent work of classicist David Sansone, who believes that all sport has a common origin and an essence that has persisted over the centuries in its role as "the ritual sacrifice of human energy." Hardy argues for a middle ground and tries to explain why some aspects of sport have changed or have become "modern" while other aspects have remained the same. He offers "Sportgeist," or the spirit of sport, as a model, and uses the American sport industry as an example of how this idea can be put to use by sport historians. Hardy examines the careers of four nineteenth-century sporting figures and their vision of the Sportgeist. Although each was different and their Sportgeists differed accordingly, Hardy concludes that certain themes from the world of the ancients still remained.

Steven A. Riess tackles myths about social mobility in American sport and shows the phenomenon to be more complex than most people believe. He questions the historical accuracy of the belief that sport was an "alternate means of vertical mobility because it was a democratic institution in which participants rose or fell solely on the basis of talent, training, and perseverance." By looking at the social, ethnic, and geographic origins of men who participated in professional boxing, baseball, football, and basketball, Riess concludes that professional sports provided an alternate route of social mobility for some athletically gifted young men, but that "the investment in time and effort is so great, and the chances of success so remote, that almost all of the hardworking athletes are misappropriating their energies." Becoming a professional athlete is a totally unrealistic goal except for a handful of young men.

Richard D. Mandell laments the fact that, despite the financial and popular dimensions of sport, it has received very little "earnest pondering." He argues that more scholars need to ask: "What does sport mean?" and attempt "to see where the spectacle fits in." This paucity of serious analysis and criticism of modern sport is particularly apparent in English-speaking countries where a myth of sport was "invented by capitalistically motivated entrepreneurs and tested and approved by the masses of industrial society." For Mandell, truly serious sport criticism arose in Germany in the late 1960s and early seventies, particularly the neo-Marxist critical school. He concludes by encouraging scholars in the field of sport history to read and understand this literature, and he recommends that selected German works be translated into English.

Allen Guttmann notes that the topic of eros and sport has always been taboo and then proceeds to debunk the myth that there is no relationship whatsoever between the two. He begins by asking the question: "How much *does* eros have to do with our human response to sports as participants and as spectators?" Guttmann analyzes how the athlete responds to his or her own body as well as the spectator's response to both performer and performance. In discussing human sexuality and physicality over the centuries, Guttmann uses scholarly articles from the fields of anthropology and psychoanalysis and he draws examples from literature, poetry, and film.

This volume of essays bodes well for the continued serious historical study of sport. The five essays, each in its own way, make readers think, and think profoundly, about what sport means to them, to their society, and to the history of mankind. The Webb lectures committee and the editors are to be commended for assembling a premier group of sport historians. Their essays incorporate all of the signs of an expanding and vital discipline.

DONALD G. KYLE

E. Norman Gardiner and the Decline of Greek Sport

IF SPORT HISTORY is the historical study of the phenomenon of sport, sport mythology includes the beliefs, legends and folklore, preconceptions and misconceptions about sport in general or about specific sports, athletes, or sporting events. The nature of mythology is exceedingly complex, but "myths" tend to fall into two groups or levels—major and minor illusions. Micro-myths are minor, specific, or local myths: traditional tales and aetiologies perpetuated by oral traditions, literature, art, and iconography. These are fictions and rationalizations generated to explain and also to entertain. They often have been expanded and embellished to the point that any historical kernel is little more than an early impetus. Macro-myths are broadly based views popularly held and transmitted: comforting stereotypes and fallacies that are largely historically inaccurate or unprovable, yet psychologically or ideologically durable and compelling. In corollary forms they transcend generations and local cultural boundaries. Theirs is the realm of universal symbols and motifs, such as the hero, the golden age, and creation. With various and varying "meanings" at different levels, these are simplifying conceptual frameworks for otherwise overwhelmingly complex and disparate realities. As historians we endeavor to refute, replace, and above all understand why both types of myths emerge and persist; but as W. H. McNeill has demonstrated, in studying diachronic human experience from man-made evidence, we cannot tell it "exactly as it was."[1] We play a game within a game; and, ironically, realistically in history—as idealistically in sport—"participating is more important than winning."

As a subdiscipline of history or sport studies, sport history has come of age and entered an increasingly revisionistic and demythologizing stage. Many popular beliefs and traditional scholarly interpretations concerning sport in various ages and cultures are being reevaluated and modified—nowhere more so than in ancient sport studies. Historically it is easiest to make "progress" demythologizing at the micro-myth level, where we often deal with specific and directly correctible myths. By research, improved techniques, and new or reexamined evidence, we are finding new "facts" and rejecting old myths. For example, we can reject the micro-myth that there was an ancient Greek marathon race: no ancient Greek would run twenty-six miles without at least delivering a message.[2] Such micro-myths stem from the macro-myth that the modern Olympics were modelled accurately on the ancient games and ideals. Progress in sport history is, in part, our improving and empirically sounder body of facts—more studies and more reliable information.

Impeding our progress in sport studies is an irritating micro-myth that sport history is an undisciplined hobby—athletic antiquarianism. For too long historians have under-studied something integral to and distinctive of ancient and all societies.[3] Sport history is too often seen, especially by academics, as a hobby for amateurs, physical educationalists, and retired jocks. Since sport is related to play (unstructured diversion involving fun), supposedly the study of sport involves undisciplined play and fun as well. This misconception has to go. Modern sport itself may be autotelic, but, like all history, sport history is studied for the end of human understanding of our past, our condition, and our nature. Sport history is especially valuable because as individuals and societies we often reveal our true selves when we engage in or watch competition. The recent explosion in both the quality and quantity of sport history proves the image of sport studies as nonscholarly diversion to be a myth, and it now leads to our increasing ability to confront sport at the macro-myth level.

It remains difficult, however, to work on the broader and deeper level of macro-myths—the level of the philosophy and not just the fact-finding of history. Here myths often relate to universal concerns—the nature of humanity, God, and process and causality in history. Here we encounter deeply-rooted ideological biases, facile or comforting generalizations, cherished ideals, symbols, icons and "-isms."[4] Such myths are even harder to deal with when there are parallel or related myths in both the culture of the historian and the culture being studied. Shared follies take on the aura of shared truths.

In general in the modern West, sport macro-myths include the idealization of sport through the ages as positive, humanistic, progressive, and "civilizing."[5] Sport is seen as socially, politically, and internationally beneficial—as an activity promoting friendship, liberalizing of views, and social mobility, and as a deterrent to actual warfare. Sport is seen as heroic and its stars as worthy of hero worship. Sport is morally didactic, teaching teamwork, initiative, and self-reliance. Sport is healthy, building body and character as well as moral well-being. Sport is refreshing—a temporary reversion to noble savagery with cathartic and enduring benefits and lasting moral elevation. Sport is sexually benign or neutral—nonerotic despite its virile men and graceful women. Sport is natural, clean and unspoiled, uncorrupted and worthy of protection from evils. Sport is amateur, at least in origin and at the level of widespread participation, not commercial. Needless to say, many of these macro-myths have suffered severely in our age of steroids, mass media, gambling, and demythologizing scholarship. Nevertheless, such myths do not die easily.

In a seminal article in 1975, H. W. Pleket said that, in addition to antiquarianism, sport studies have suffered from a "classicist bias," a preference for amateurism, and a tendency to impose rise and fall patterns.[6] Such mythologizing misconceptions and preconceptions about Greek sport have had their most influential protagonist in E. Norman Gardiner (1864–1930). While not the originator of the idea, Gardiner has greatly contributed academically to the persistence over the decades of the notion that ancient Greek sport experienced a well-defined historical decline as a consequence of "excess" and the weakening of an ideal. Gardiner's mythology was influenced by his own experience as an athlete, classicist, and schoolteacher, as well as by his Victorian cultural milieu, his mentors, and his ancient sources.

Even at my first casual reading of Gardiner as a graduate student, I felt his schema of Greek sport was reductionistic and I did not care for the personality behind the pages. For Gardiner, sport reached its height and actualized its ideal in the organized but amateur Panhellenic games. Soon, however, sport fell victim to its own popularity and started to deteriorate in the second half of the fifth century B.C., with a dangerous expansion of athletic festivals and honors for victors leading to over-competition and professionalism. Gardiner presents decline and fall as the historical process, and professionalism as the historical proof of that process.

Gardiner's editorial comments showed him to be an idealist dreaming of a golden age, and a moralist condemning a fall from grace. He also seemed a social elitist and at times even a racist. Nevertheless, as my dissertation topic on ancient athletics emerged, I came to delight in Gardiner. At the time I did not care *why* he was biased—I was grateful that he was. Here was a monumental straw man and graduate school had just honed my incendiary skills. Fortunately, both I as a historian, and ancient sport studies as a discipline, have matured somewhat in recent years. The study of ancient sport is now moving past Gardiner to a point where, beyond simply rejecting many of his micro-myths, we need better to understand his macro-mythology. Demythologizing entails refutation but also explication.

In terms of his domination of the field, and his scholarship, style, and sincerity, Gardiner is to the supposed decline of Greek sport what Gibbon has been to the "decline and fall" of the Roman Empire. Almost sixty years after his death Gardiner's publications remain standard reference works.[7] Most recent evaluations of Gardiner have been generally positive, despite reservations about his biases and outdated archaeology. In 1978 Stephen G. Miller wrote:

> The timelessness of Gardiner's work lies, then, partly in his enormous learning. It lies even more, however, in his ability to write intelligibly for both the interested layman and the specialized scholar. . . . His learning sits gracefully upon his lucid prose, and one recognizes that Gardiner knew his subject matter intimately, cared for it tremendously, and wanted to share it generously.[8]

For decades Gardiner was authoritative and his follower H. A. Harris continued in the same vein, but the tarnished modern Olympics and the increasingly professional and spectacular nature of modern sport eventually made Gardiner's ideals seem out of place. Since the mid-1970s Gardiner has been challenged more and more, by I. Weiler, H. W. Pleket, M. B. Poliakoff, and others on the sociology, origins, and even the techniques of Greek sport. Scathing criticism of Gardiner came in 1984 from David C. Young, a major contributor to the demythologizing of Greek and Olympic sport history. Young sees Gardiner as an absolutely dedicated amateurist and as an influential popularizer of the Olympist mythology. In Young's eyes Gardiner is a poor and not a disinterested historian with "cavalier historical analogies" and weak interpretations of evidence. A "classical scholar of the second rank," Gardiner indulged in "chronological legerdemain"—misdating persons and events to champion a delusive conspiracy.[9]

Young has admirably exposed the mythological substructure of modern Olympism, but on Gardiner his tone is rather intolerant. There is a baby in the bathwater. Where Young sees conspiracy and class warfare, I also see mythology and problems endemic to sport history. Aspects of Gardiner's life and world made it virtually impossible for him to be objective about sport or Greece. We need to understand what Gardiner brought to, put in, and found in the history of Greek sport. To that end this paper examines and attempts to explain Gardiner's remarkable approach to sport history by discussing his life, works, and ideas on Greek sport, and by relating those ideas to Gardiner's cultural milieu and the ancient materials he used.

GARDINER'S LIFE, WORKS, AND IDEAS ON GREEK SPORT

E. Norman Gardiner was born on January 16, 1864, the only son of the Reverend Edward Imber Gardiner of Buckingham, who was an Oxford M.A. graduate of Magdellan Hall in 1864 and became rector of Radwell in Hertsfordshire in 1882. The younger Gardiner won a scholarship, went away to public school at Marlborough, matriculated in 1883, and went to Corpus Christi College, Oxford, as an exhibitioner (a student maintained by a donated allowance). He received second class honors in the classical schools and earned a B.A. and M.A. by 1890, and ultimately a D. Litt. by 1925.[10] At Oxford Gardiner was a rower in several crews for Corpus Christi, and his obituary in *The Times* mentions that he played rugby football for Devonshire from "1887 to 1900" and for the Western Counties in 1888–89.[11] After three years as master at Newton College, Gardiner settled down in 1890 at Epsom College in Surrey to remain there, as a house master and then as assistant master (for some 25 years), until his retirement to Oxford in 1925.

Around 1900 Gardiner took up serious research on ancient sport. He joined the prestigious and influential Society for the Promotion of Hellenic Studies in 1902 and published his first of several articles in the *Journal of Hellenic Studies* (JHS) in 1903.[12] Lists of members and officers of the Hellenic Society published in *JHS* show that he became a member of its council in 1906 and that he died as a member of the council of 1930–31. Minutes from the proceedings of the society for 1930–31 note Gardiner's death as a loss to the society and its council.[13]

Widespread concern about challenges to classical education led the society in 1921–22 to establish the Committee on the Further Popularisation of the Classics, commonly known as the Popularisation Committee. Gardiner served on this ten-person committee with classicists such as J. D. Beazley, H. Last, and P. N. Ure. In the 1920s the committee created a new policy for student associate memberships, arranged a course of popular lectures by distinguished scholars, and issued three advisory pamphlets. Gardiner also personally contributed a lecture text for a slide set on "Olympia and Greek Athletics."[14] Actively combating the decline of classical studies at all levels, Gardiner also joined the Roman Society and the Classical Association. In retirement at Oxford, he appears in the listings of the officers of the Classical Association as one of the honourable secretaries in 1926, a position he held until his death.[15]

Gardiner died on October 20, 1930, at his beloved Oxford, leaving behind no family, a net estate of 15,679 pounds, and a considerable legacy for ancient sport studies.[16] As the journal of the Classical Association, the *Classical Review* of December, 1930 included an obituary notice, "From a correspondent," which comments that, "in a word, Dr. Gardiner saved his theme from the Reallexicographers by making it a living and attractive subject." The notice depicts Gardiner as a quiet man, "a diligent and interesting specialist" with a "simple and detached manner": "His interesting but unassuming personality and his obvious dislike for polemics mark him out as an unusual man whom it was a privilege to have as a friend."[17] This is not quite the image of Gardiner that comes across in his works, but he clearly was a member of a circle of devoted friends and scholarly colleagues. His prefaces acknowledge eminent Hellenists including P. Gardner, B. Ashmole, and J. D. Beazley. The notice adds, "As one of the Secretaries [of the Classical Association], he was both vigorous and sympathetic. In Roman archaeology, as in Greek, he was always ready to help and encourage all enterprise and research." Immediately following the notice is a comment by the association: "As Secretary of the Classical Association he found many ways of placing the *Classical Review*, and the interests of classical learning in the widest sense, in his debt."

As we shall see below, Gardiner was strongly influenced by his public school and university education, his cultural environment, and his intellectual circle. Central to understanding Gardiner, I believe, is his probable self-perception first and foremost as a teacher, secondly as a scholar, and thirdly as a former athlete.[18] For good and ill, Gardiner, by virtue of his education and occupation, was a Victorian gentleman and a Hellenist. His comments on Greece, sport, and education were not fully objective, nor were they so intended.

Understanding Gardiner entails examining all his publications concerning his historiography (aims and methods), his mythology (biases and ideology), and his sources (both modern and ancient). In all Gardiner produced three books, two edited schoolboy texts, fifteen articles, and various book reviews (see appendix). Between 1903 and 1907 he published nine lengthy articles in the *Journal of Hellenic Studies* on various Greek athletic events and related technical problems.[19] Amounting to more than 170 pages, these articles represent a remarkable output. In them Gardiner emerges as an idealistic and sometimes arrogant scholar who could be intolerant in dealing with the works of others. When discussing athletic techniques, he frequently asserts the value of practical experience, modern comparisons, and re-creations. He does not explicitly mention his own athletic experience, but he finds lack of experience a flaw in others.[20] The myths of amateurism and deline appear early in these early articles; both wrestling and the *pankration* are said to decline from the use of skill and grace to use of mere strength and increasing brutality.[21] The theme of decline is far more overt when Gardiner discusses heavy events than when he treats track and field, but not as overt as it would be later in his books, for here Gardiner was still working on technical questions more than historical patterns.

Unfortunately overshadowed by his more popular *Athletics of the Ancient World* (AAW) of 1930, *Greek Athletic Sports and Festivals* (GASF) of 1910 is the work in which Gardiner made his greatest academic contributions and his most fully documented articulation of his mythology of rise and fall. His preface to *GASF* explains his intention of combining technical or archaeological matters with an historical overview of Greek athletics. He arranged his chapters in order "to bring out the historical aspect of the subject, an aspect which is completely obscured in most of our text-books." Gardiner says he writes because there is no existing work on the subject in English, because of recent archaeological discoveries, and because of the relevance for modern Britain of the Greek sporting experience.[22] Not the first or last historian to claim but to fall short of a very high level of historiographical integrity, Gardiner declares that he has formed his own judgements and that his work is accurate.[23] Gardiner espouses cautious and principled research, but he is certain about the causes, chronology, and results of the decline of Greek sport.

In 1912 his article "Panathenaic Amphorae" presented a specialized discussion of Panathenaic amphorae as evidence for sport. Here he attacks the theories of von Brauchitsch as "the merest moonshine" and argues, in part from the vases, that Athenian athletics declined through the latter part of the fifth century.[24] In "The Alleged Kingship of the Olympic Victor" of 1916, as he would do later, he credits the origin of Greek athletics to the human love of play and fighting, a secular impulse characteristic of northerners (by this, Gardiner means Europeans) and early societies.[25] The idea that early sport was essentially military and practical was carried over from GASF and would recur in AAW. In 1920 Gardiner published a light but revealing encomium on the work of a modern Canadian artist, Dr. R. Tait McKenzie. He applauds McKenzie's revival of athletic sculpture and suggests that modern artists can learn from these efforts to represent the ideal athlete in form and in action. Gardiner's enthusiasm for his "friend" spilled over into praiseful references and illustrations in AAW.[26]

Olympia. Its History and Remains of 1925 followed GASF in combining technical (archaeological/topographical) and historical chapters. It made the results of recent German archaeological work at Olympia available for English readers, and it traced the history of Olympia and the festival. The work lacked much originality, but through detailed archaeological reporting and good illustrations it performed a valuable and enduring service. The book is notable for Gardiner's idealization of Olympia (with the nationalistic theme of Panhellenism), for the racial myth of innate athletic prowess among northern peoples, and for the continued myth of decline.[27]

As Gardiner entered his sixth decade, his productivity did not diminish. It is revealing that even though he was now an established authority on sport, he took time in 1927–28 to edit selections from Livy and Virgil—simple instructional texts for public schoolboys. In Extracts from Livy, a new edition of Lee-Warner's work, Gardiner's aim was to enable the young student "to read with fair rapidity" and "to appreciate Livy's wonderful power of storytelling;"[28] but Livy's moralizing on the decline of Italian natural vigor was attractive too. Gardiner's *Selections from Virgil's Eclogues and Georgics* was a well-received anthology with illustrations, notes and vocabulary.[29] Virgil's bucolic works seem appropriate for someone who viewed himself as a country gentleman, and Gardiner clearly sympathizes with Virgil's love of nature and the countryside.[30] It is interesting that in *Virgil* Gardiner atypically mentions Christianity.[31] Gardiner was a clergyman's son but he went away to school and embraced Humanistic Hellenism (see below). He probably was a knowledgeable and practicing Christian, but religion was not a major factor in his work.

Athletics of the Ancient World of 1930 has found Gardiner's widest audience, including use as a textbook. In the preface he declares his aim of giving "a short and simple account of the history and practice of athletics in the ancient world which will appeal to all who are interested in athletics and be of use to students of the past."[32] This was to be a "shorter and simpler" work (still over three hundred pages in reprint editions), but "no mere abridgement of my earlier book." However, *AAW is* largely an abridgement, with paraphrases and echoes. In retirement at Oxford, Gardiner took his myths as established truths and he articulated their elements and sources less fully.

In 1929 Gardiner had published for the first time in the *Classical Review* with his "Regulations for a Local Sports Meeting," a discussion of an inscription from Asia Minor. He probably was especially attracted by one regulation evidently intended "to prevent some pot-hunting professional coming in and carrying off the prizes."[33] Shortly after Gardiner's death the *CR* published his "A School in Ptolemaic Egypt," a brief discussion of two papyri recording arrangements for the training of a young athlete.[34] Again the chance to discuss professionalism perhaps was the stimulus: "Athletics in the third century B.C. was a profitable profession. Parents sending a boy to school would exhort the teacher to turn him into an athlete just as they sometimes today exhort the schoolmaster to teach their boys cricket, though not for quite the same motive."[35] Even from the grave, Gardiner was offering parallels and lessons from antiquity. We should not be blind to Gardiner's faults, including arrogance and dogmatism, but his scholarly productivity remains impressive. On questions of athletic technique he was deservedly recognized as *the* English expert, but major problems occur when Gardiner deals with moral or diachronic issues.

Gardiner's ideas deserve examination in detail, especially those in *GASF*, which offers the fullest and best documented version of his schema of the rise and fall of Greek sport. The pattern is dramatic and tragic: from natural roots sport comes of age as a larger-than-life hero with the tragic flaw of its own popularity leading to excess and hero worship. Gibbon felt Rome fell due to its immoderate greatness, and Gardiner sees the decline of sport as triggered by its excess popularity. Despite tragic warnings for moderation, sport strays from the pure ideal, and the weakened spirit allows corruption and excess. Specialization and professionalism signal the start of a long and sorrowful decline.

GASF establishes Gardiner's ideas on the beginning and early stages of Greek sport as a phenomenon arising from natural, secular origins and the agonal spirit of the "tall fair-haired" northern races. Out of weak ethnology or contemporary racism, Gardiner simply rejects the notion of Minoan athletics: the Greeks were the only "truly athletic nation of antiquity."[36] In his laudatory treatment of Homeric sport in *GASF*, Gardiner sees the essentials of the Greek ideal as already present, and as a natural expression of martial spirit and the love of effort. "Aristocratic and spontaneous" with no organized training, Homeric sport was part of the education of boys and the recreation of men, with excellence belonging to the nobles. For Gardiner this was sport on the rise towards the ideal but still lacking organized competitions and facilities. He presents the development of sport after Homer as involving an association with festivals. At the start of the sixth century Olympia had "a unique position as the national festival of Hellas"; it was a force for unity and a model for other festivals. With Olympia leading and others following, sport circa 500 B.C. was still joyful recreation but it had become more organized, popular, and "democratic."[37]

For Gardiner, the true Greek athletic ideal was briefly and partially realized in the fifth century; it was both promoted by and expressed in athletic art and poetry. The idea of *paideia* or education is central to Gardiner's ideology; for him Greek sport and education were harmonious, moral, and joyful. "In the Periclean age, we cannot distinguish between the athlete and the ephebos. Every educated youth is an athlete, and every athlete is an educated youth and a citizen of a free state."[38] The idea recurs in *AAW*: "To cultivate mind and body alike, to keep the balance between music and gymnastic, was the ideal of Greek education, but like all ideals it is hard to realize." The use of the present tense—that the ideal *is* hard to realize—is deliberate: Gardiner's model expression of the athletic ideal was the young Greek athlete whom he analogized to the British schoolboy.[39]

When Gardiner applauds early sport and the athletic ideal he often uses the image of sport as a fresh air, outdoor recreation with positive benefits. Early gymnasia in towns were for exercising, not athletic training: "The bulk of the population living an open-air country life in which war, hunting, and games played a considerable part, had no need of training." Early Greek athletics and education are idealized as practical for military purposes: "The athletic ideal of Greece is largely due to the practical character of Greek athletics. . . . Every Greek was a soldier, physical fitness was a necessity to him, and his athletic exercises were admirably calculated to produce this fitness."[40] Sport brought fitness and military preparedness, which brought victory in the Persian wars, which fostered Panhellenism, which fostered athletics. It was too good to last.

The early games had been spontaneous and recreational but the potential for "evils" existed early on; and as the "spirit" weakened, sport strayed from the moderate ideal, and corruption set in during the fifth century. Popularity led to excess honors and thence over-competition, specialization, and technical training.

> The result of specialization is professionalism. There is a point in any sport or game where it becomes over-developed, and competition too severe, for it to serve its true purpose of providing exercise or recreation for the many. It becomes the monopoly of the few who can afford the time or money to acquire excellence, while the rest, despairing of any measure of success, prefer the role of spectators. When the rewards of success are sufficient there arises a professional class, and when professionalism is once established the amateur can no longer compete with the professional.[41]

Over-competition was "fatal to the true amateur spirit." Instead of athletics remaining "a recreation and a training for war, they became an end in themselves."

> Thus, early in the fifth century there arose "the pothunter," who spent most of his time travelling from city to city, picking up prizes. . . . For such a man athletics were no longer a recreation, but an absorbing occupation which left little time for other duties. When the "Shamateur" makes his appearance, professionalism is not far off.[42]

Performances improved but specialization and professionalism, the signs of a mortally wounded spirit, heralded a long, sorrowful decline. Soon a class of professionals monopolized and degraded sport socially and morally. Gardiner claims that, although the athletic ideal continued to have some influence at Olympia, in the age of decline professionals obsessed with records competed for profit, and idle, ill-fit masses simply watched. Decline was rampant by 400 and fully entrenched after 338 B.C. "Thus within a century the whole character of Greek athletics was completely changed. From this time there is little to record save that all the evils which we have described grew more and more pronounced."[43]

Openly moralistic and dogmatic, Gardiner's rhetoric combines a classicist's scenario of tragic rise and fall with a Victorian gentleman's value-laden vocabulary. Good things include: natural, amateur, aristocratic, healthy, moral, vigor, youth, harmony, and peace. Bad items include: luxury, excess, strife, philistine, professional, pale, and evil. Friendly sporting rivalry was pure, masculine, participatory, and nationalistic; it was moderate, moral, and graceful rather than brutal, commercial, or corrupt.[44] Gardiner feels that "excess," in popularity or preparations, ruins sport; it necessarily brings "nemesis."

> Nowhere is excess more dangerous than in athletics, and the charm of poetry and art must not blind us to that element of exaggeration which existed in the hero-worship of the athlete. The nemesis of excess in athletics is specialization, specialization begets professionalism, and professionalism is the death of all true sport.[45]

Note that excess precedes and brings about professionalism; Gardiner has a dramatic concept of historical process as well as an abhorrence for professionalism.

Despite Gardiner's faith in his mythology of decline, historically the concept of decline is very problematic. By definition and etymology "decline" (*declinatio*) means a pattern of negative change over time, a deterioration or a leaning/sloping/bending away from an earlier state, posture, or condition. Decline, or progress, must be argued relative to something and via some criteria, and the soundest way to measure decline is in value-free quantitative terms, such as measurements of resources or population, preferably in large samplings. We must first know the status of the subject before, during, and after a time period. Perspective and criteria are all-important: in the Late Roman Empire imperial strength diminished but Christianity grew. A particular focus or qualitative criteria may simply indicate value judgements or mythology (held by the historian or the culture under study—or both).

Gardiner's chronology of decline is clear but forced. After the long rise of Greek sport, the brief age of the ideal (ca. 500–440 B.C.) is followed by increasing specialization and professionalism (ca. 440–338). Decline is outright from 338 B.C. to A.D. 393. This bald rise and fall schema is contrary to current conceptualizations of major developments in ancient history. Even studies of the "decline and fall" of the Roman Empire now avoid strict periodization: they speak of "transformation," "fusion," and even the "myth" of the fall of Rome.[46] Of course Greek sport experienced historical change, but we no longer buy Gardiner's simple schema of a fifth-century crisis leading to a long, consistent decline.[47]

Gardiner's criteria and termini for decline were not actual historical circumstances in sport—not revenues, records, or numbers of participants. He admits that during decline, crowds, participation, performances, facilities, and festivals persisted and expanded.[48] Gardiner dates and asserts decline on the basis of selected examples from art and literature, Greek military history, and the supposed shift to professionalism. He paints the history of an ideal so pure that it never really existed. He feels its best actualization came under the Panhellenic and "purifying influence of the enthusiasm evoked by the war with Persia." The "noblest tribute" to the ideal was the athletic art and poetry it inspired. The date 440 is the turning point for Gardiner largely because by that time Pindar and Myron had stopped writing victory odes and making athletic sculpture.[49] After 440 Gardiner sees increasing criticism of sport in literature, and the Peloponnesian War replaces Panhellenism.[50] Hence, for Gardiner, the athletic ideal that had fostered earlier unity and greatness *must* have collapsed. This simply is poor history, but it is also understandable mythologizing when one considers the cultural context of Gardiner's life.

CULTURAL AND MYTHOLOGICAL INFLUENCES ON GARDINER

In the course of his education and career Gardiner espoused three mutually reinforcing ideologies about games and education, athletics, and the relevance of ancient Greece for the modern world: athleticism, amateurism, and Victorian Humanistic Hellenism. Understanding Gardiner's works, ideas, and influence entails examining each of these three mythologies and their combined influence on Gardiner.

Athleticism

An early and continuous mythological stream flowing through Gardiner's life and works is the ideology of athleticism concerning education and sport, whereby games are seen to inspire virtue and manliness. J. A. Mangan shows that athleticism greatly influenced British public schools from about 1860 to the 1940s.

> Physical exercise was taken, considerably and compulsorily, in the sincere belief of many, however romantic, misplaced or myopic, that it was a highly effective means of inculcating valuable instrumental and impressive educational goals: physical and moral courage, loyalty and co-operation, the capacity to act fairly and take defeat well, the ability to both command and obey.[51]

The origins of athleticism lay with various headmasters, notably C. J. Vaughn at Harrow, who introduced games for various reasons, including discipline, and then developed a rationalizing ideology. The movement spread to and from the universities; they received it from the schools and disseminated it further, since many schoolmasters and most diplomats came from Oxford or Cambridge. As Mangan explains, under the influence of imperialism, athleticism involved an ironic combination of Christian gentility and Social Darwinism. It combined antithetical values: "success, aggression, and ruthlessness, yet victory within the rules, courtesy in triumph, compassion for the defeated." Widely supported by parents, press, and public, athleticism connected muscular Christianity with the success of the British Empire via physical and moral vigor.[52]

The ideology of athleticism was fortified by symbolism, rituals, vocabulary, and rhetoric. Mangan sees four categories of verbal symbols:

the rhetoric of cohesion, of sexual identity, of patriotism, and above all of morality. Unity meant solidarity and cohesion. Manliness meant "asexual manliness": boys were to be manly in physique but they were not to have sexual knowledge or experience. Patriotism involved martial duty with games as a metaphor for war. Morality meant games built moral fiber; games were a preparation for the game of life. The rhetoric of athleticism bolstered the belief in Anglo-Saxon moral superiority via games, and it drew on the playing field for inspiration. "Metaphor, manners and myth went hand in hand."[53]

Gardiner is tied to athleticism by his biography, ideology, and rhetoric. His public school, Marlborough, was one of Mangan's case studies. Marlborough was an example of a proprietary school, which was one financed initially by shareholders who purchased the right to nominate students. Established in 1843 mainly for the sons of clergymen, Marlborough played an important role in the development of athleticism. G. E. L. Cotton, headmaster from 1852 to 1858, introduced games, appointed young games players as masters to draw students to the playing fields, and preached the moral and physical benefits of games. Nevertheless, several Marlborough headmasters favored balance and moderation. G. C. Bell (1876–1903), headmaster over Gardiner, was critical of the games ethos. The curriculum remained primarily classical and there was less anti-intellectualism than elsewhere: ". . . in all probability Marlborough was the most intellectual, and contained the most academically able boys, of the schools under consideration, yet here the new passion for the games field was very evident."[54]

After Marlborough Gardiner went to an athleticized Oxford and then carried athleticism into his teaching career at Epsom, a new school on Thomas Arnold's model and catering to the sons of doctors. Gardiner was hired by headmaster Rev. T. N. H. Smith-Pearse (1889–1914), "a confirmed classicist" under whom Epsom become a major school as the number of boys more than doubled.[55] Smith-Pearse probably was attracted to Gardiner by his background in rugby as well as in classics. Gardiner thus typifies what Mangan calls the "process of circular causality":

> The successful games player at school flourished in the same capacity at the university and then returned to school as lauded assistant master to set another generation of devotees along the same route. Thus a cycle

of "schoolboy sportsman, university sportsman and schoolmaster sports-man was created."[56]

Gardiner became a schoolmaster sportsman, and with the insularity of his career, his values remained filtered by athleticism.

That athleticism vitiated Gardiner's works is all too obvious. Cherishing its values and rhetoric, Gardiner applauds the "friendly rivalry," "effort," and asexual masculine virtue of uncorrupted sport in early Greece as in English schools. Gardiner felt sport was educative but he was against excessive preparations or trained expertise. He opposed separating athletics from physical education and he favorably contrasts athletic education and competition with scientific physical education, both ancient and modern.[57]

In the post-Boer War era, Gardiner and athleticists argued that games aid military preparedness.

> The defeat of Persia not only gave a fresh impulse to the Panhellenic festivals: it raised athletic training into a national duty. The consciousness of a great danger safely past arouses a nation to a sense of its military and physical needs. We can remember only a few years ago the growth of rifle clubs, the cry for military and physical training that followed the Boer war.[58]

Athleticists exhorted boys to "play the game" and to learn moral lessons through games as a preparation for the "game of life." In Gardiner's words:

> Physical training is a valuable part of education and necessary in artificial conditions of life. But physical training is not sport, nor can it ever take the place of sport. There is no joy in it. It may develop the body and impart habits of discipline, but it cannot impart those higher qualities—courage, endurance, self-control, courtesy—qualities which are developed by our own games and by such manly sports as boxing and wrestling when conducted in the true spirit of manly rivalry for the pure joy of the contest; it cannot train boys "to play the game" in the battle of life.[59]

Like the Masters of Trinity and Caius admonishing Abrahams in the 1981 film *Chariots of Fire*, Gardiner felt sport was a matter of spirit not science, games not greed.

Victorian athleticism explains much about Gardiner and his work. It reinforced his notions of virtuous, friendly rivalry, asexual masculinity, and the practicality of games as preparation for war and citizenship. Nationalism and imperialism contributed to Gardiner's racial notion that northerners were better by nature and by games. Teaching the sons of doctors at Epsom only increased Gardiner's concern for "health" and "education." As a teacher he attended to the bodies, minds, and morality of youths.

Amateurism

The second macro-myth prominent in Gardiner's life and works is amateurism, the view that proper sport is free of money and professionalism. David C. Young has rejected Gardiner's soon traditional notions that early Greek athletes were all idealistic, noble amateurs, and that athletics degenerated with professionalism in the fifth century B.C. He exposes Greek amateurism as a myth based on modern and unsatisfactory rather than ancient and reliable works, a myth in the sense of a "universal belief" and also in the sense of a comforting falsehood held by Olympists. Ancient athletes regularly competed for valuable prizes, Olympic victory brought wealth, and no stigma or word existed for "professional": the Greeks lacked both the ideology and the vocabulary of amateurism. Young offers evidence to deny Gardiner's thesis: stories Gardiner used to illustrate the evils of later professionalism actually belong to the sixth-century age of supposed amateurism. "The methodology is . . . preposterous. . . . It recurs repeatedly and consistently, misleading readers far worse than ordinary sloppy scholarship." [60]

Young presents our modern notion of Greek sport as a product of amateurist class bias and bad scholarship. Providing a history of the Olympist myth of Greek amateurism from nineteenth-century roots, Young finds the origin of the amateurist (and shortly the Olympist) myth specifically in J. P. Mahaffy; and Young sees Percy Gardner as the crucial link in the transmission of amateurism from Mahaffy and Casper Whitney to Gardiner, Paul Shorey, Coubertin, Brundage, and others. [61] Gardiner undoubtedly was influenced by Gardner but he also had read Mahaffy directly. Gardiner and Mahaffy agree in seeing the early Greeks as amateurs, intensive training as harmful, and later professionals as despicable. Gardiner would later echo Mahaffy's fears that

cricket and boating were being "vulgarized by the invasion of the professional spirit," which did not support "sport for its own sake."[62]

As Young shows, Percy Gardner, Gardiner's mentor, was a staunch
amateurist for whom "decline" meant the participation of the working
classes. "Gardner's history of Greece is really nothing other than the
history of Anglo-American sports from the 1860's to the 1890's seen
through the gentleman amateur's eye." As Young notes, Gardiner admits the influence of Gardner:

> It is a fitting circumstance that this book should have been produced
> under the auspices of Professor Percy Gardner, seeing that he was uncon-
> sciously the originator of it. My interest in the subject was first aroused by
> the chapter on Olympia in his *New Chapters from Greek History* (sic),
> which I read on my return from a cruise on the "Argonaut," in the course
> of which I had visited Olympia. Professor Gardner has read the book both
> in manuscript and in proof, and many improvements are due to his
> suggestions.[63]

Obviously Gardiner and Gardner shared numerous value judgements
and drew similar "lessons" from Greek sport.[64] For example, like
Gardner, Gardiner condemns professionalism:

> The evil effects of professionalism are worst in those fighting events, box-
> ing, wrestling and pankration, where the feeling of aidos or honour is most
> essential. Here again the history of modern sport tells the same tale.
> Wrestling which was once a national sport in England has been killed by
> professionalism. . . . When a boxer will not fight unless he is guaranteed a
> huge purse whether he wins or loses he forfeits all claim to be called a
> sportsman.[65]

Young demonstrates clearly that Gardiner "borrowed" ideas from
the amateurists, and he effectively debunks the amateurist elements of
the myth of decline. However, amateurism was not the only opera-
tional myth about sport and Greece in Gardiner's England,[66] and Gardiner was no myopic myrmidon. He could and did disagree with his
mentors, and he increasingly turned to better German and English
sources.[67] Also it is understandable that he would emulate Gardner,
who was a senior classicist, formerly with the British Museum, and
who had been Lincoln and Merton Professor of Classical Archaeology
and Art at Oxford, Late Disney Professor of Archaeology at Cambridge, editor of *JHS* (1880–87), and president of the Hellenic Society

(1906–10). The nineteenth century laid less emphasis than we do on originality. Fleshing out the ideas of a master was seen as worthwhile. Gardiner filled in and bolstered the chronological schema, going into technical points and beyond Olympia. He amassed and discussed more evidence on sport than any other British scholar.

Gardiner was influenced by amateurist scholars, but he also had a personal involvement. Born two years before the establishment of the Amateur Athletic Club, he was an amateur school athlete and rugby player. His lifetime saw the rise and fall of the amateurist movement and the early decades of the fledgling modern Olympics.[68] Gardiner was a participant and advocate of amateur sport, and the history of sports in contemporary England disturbed him deeply.

> Of the evils of professionalism this is no place to speak. . . . The history of football during the last two years is ominous. On the one hand we see the leading amateur clubs revolting from the tyranny of a Football Association conducted in the interests of joint-stock companies masquerading as Football Clubs; on the other hand we see the professional players forming a trades-union to protect themselves against the tyranny of this same commercialism. The Rugby Union has struggled manfully to uphold the purity of the game. . . . Under these circumstances the history of the decline of Greek athletics is an object-lesson full of instruction.[69]

Gardiner was lamenting the modernization of British football. After the development of ball games under the influence of the public schools, and the bifurcation of rugby and soccer, "professional" soccer began with the recruitment and payment of (especially Scottish) players. Separate amateur and professional leagues were established within the Football Association in 1885; amateur clubs could no longer compete with professionals, and "football mania" and massive spectatorship became the norm. During Gardiner's playing years the Rugby Union rejected professionalism as unacceptable but by the turn of the century rugby was split between professionals in the industrial north and educated amateurs in the south. Given such developments, Gardiner's comments are pointed and topical. He was comparing and confusing ancient and modern developments.[70]

Interestingly enough, while an ardent amateurist, Gardiner was not a great admirer of Coubertin's revived Olympics. He applauded their professed ideals but he was critical of the authenticity of technical aspects of the events.[71] Above all, he was skeptical about the dangers of over-competition.

> The promoters of these games were inspired by the ideal of ancient Greece, and wished to establish a great international athletic meeting which would be for the nations of the world what Olympia was for Greece. We must all sympathize with their aspirations. Unfortunately they do not seem to have realized the full lesson of Greek athletics, nor did they realize the dangers of competition on so vast a scale. . . . The experience of recent years has taught us that international competitions do not always make for amity, and do not always promote amateur sport. The events of the last Olympic games . . . have gone far to justify the forebodings of those who feared that one of the chief results of such a competition would be an increase in professionalism.[72]

Perhaps Gardiner may be forgiven some reservations about the modern Olympics, especially those of 1908 in London, which historians have called "the battle of Shepherd's Bush" because of the numerous protests against the British officiating. The *New York Times* said of these games that "as a means of promoting international friendship it has been a deplorable failure."[73] More and more the games of the English schoolboy seemed to be the only bastion of pure sport left for Gardiner.

Victorian Humanistic Hellenism

The third and most pervasive and inclusive cultural influence on Gardiner was "Victorian Humanistic Hellenism," a widespread nineteenth-century intellectual enthusiasm for ancient Greece. Aware of themselves in a world in transition with industrialism, and political and moral change, Victorian intellectuals had a fin de siècle preoccupation with decadence and they increasingly revered ancient Greece as a humane and humanizing civilization.[74] Frank M. Turner characterizes the Victorian approach to Greece as "prescriptive" and "selective": "The Victorian study of the Greek heritage occurred in an arena of thoroughly engaged scholarship and writing. Disinterested or dispassionate criticism was simply not the order of the day." Hellenists hoped that proper study of classical art, literature, poetry, and politics could teach proper values and bring inner peace and social harmony to contemporary society. Mostly conservatives and elitists, Hellenists generally opposed excessive commercialism, individualism, moral relativism, political radicalism, materialism, and aspects of pluralism in society.

They imposed their concerns, ideology, and traditional morality and gentility on the Greeks. Then in turn they used these Victorian Greeks as rationalizations or lessons for aspects of contemporary life. The Victorians were not the only culture to view the past through the present but they were remarkably intense and overt in doing so.[75]

A key figure in the Hellenist idealization of Greek culture as the embodiment of proper Victorian values is Matthew Arnold (1822–88). Turner shows how Arnold retrojected British humanistic values onto the Greeks, idealizing them, especially in the period 530–430 B.C., as beautiful, rational, placid, and unified—a culture of "sweetness and light"—as a means to denounce the individualism, liberalism, and utilitarianism of contemporary "barbarians" and "philistines." In seeing fifth-century Greece as relevant and modern, Matthew Arnold was influenced by the theory of historical cycles of his father, Thomas Arnold (1795–1842), who felt that all nations developed through organic stages comparable to those of individual human growth, maturation, and decay. Widely believing in patterns of rise and fall, growth and decay, Victorians tended to see Greek literature and history as rising and falling in a parabola with a brief blaze and rapid decline.[76] Gardiner was not exceptional in his myth of decline or in his idealism about Greek sport and art.

The Hellenists' approach to Greek art is shown in the careers of the brothers Percy and Ernest Gardner, who together condemned the harshness and excesses of contemporary art and urged the emulation of the perceived purity, strength, and reserve of Greek sculpture. Indebted heavily to the ideas of J. J. Winckelmann, the father of German Hellenism, the Gardners interpreted Greek art idealistically and believed in the influence of physical climate and cultural environment on the Greek artistic achievement. The fine air, sunshine, and exercises of the Greeks allowed artists to observe nude athletes in the gymnasia, select the best parts to embody an ideal of beauty, and so reinforce a communal appreciation of beauty. The Gardners also applied the rise and fall organic pattern to Greek art and felt that political independence was essential for ideal art and sport.[77]

Profoundly influenced by his education, mentors, and scholarly associates, especially in the Hellenic Society, Gardiner applied Hellenist inclinations to ancient sport and saw a singular Greek athletic ideal, the decline of which offered lessons for England.[78] Like other classicists, even great ones like Jebb, Jowett, and Grote, Gardiner used contemporary terms, categories, and concerns in his studies. He openly pushed analogies and studied Greek sport not for its own sake but for contemporary relevance and value. Any reader of Gardiner will agree that his works abound in typical Hellenist themes of natural beauty and serenity, fresh air, youthfulness, and the importance of independence. His rhetoric and the premises of his chronological schema, as discussed above, are typically Victorian. His parallel of English schoolboys to Greek youths and their statues was a Victorian commonplace.[79] The evils and excesses of athletics attacked by Gardiner were those of contemporary English society: professionalism was but one facet of a broad pattern of perceived decline or falling away from an ideal state.

Sport and decline have too often formed a playing field for biases and ideologies; and Gardiner's Hellenism is similar to what Patrick Brantlinger calls "negative classicism": an elitist modern mythology or view of history that sees extensions of mass or popular culture, as in spectator sports, as leading to the decline of empires or cultures. Brantlinger points out inconsistencies in the negative classicism of nineteenth-century liberals, like Thomas Arnold, who favored democratization through education but not egalitarianism or great social disruption. They felt that ideally the masses could be enculturated, but they doubted the compatibility of democracy with cultural greatness. "Instead of their elevation through a wholesome absorption of 'high culture,' 'the masses,' it was often feared, would drag everything down to their own level, perhaps smashing the very machinery of civilization in the process."[80] Modern sport and mass culture might bring popular access and better skills but, by what Brantlinger calls "the paradox of progress as decadence," they were still seen as decline. The paradox of progress as decadence clarifies inconsistencies in Gardiner. He considered Olympia democratic and Greece a nation of athletes, but when commoners participated, Gardiner feared corruption and debasement to the commoner's unhealthy level of materialism and spectatorship.[81] Commoners should have the right to compete in the games, but they should not actually do so; excellence and victory properly were the preserve of the better classes. In Gardiner's mind, when commoners competed and nobles withdrew, Greek civilization began to degenerate.

Even though anthropology and historicism were taking ancient studies in other directions during his lifetime, Gardiner's historical model remained an Arnoldian idealistic and organic one: Greek sport had an ideal or spirit from early times, it grew to full but brief realization at the top of the parabola, and then when the spirit weakened, a decline or falling away set in. Gardiner shared in the Victorian fin de siècle attitude concerning the empire, morality, sport and more, and his inclinations understandably hardened as he aged.

GARDINER'S ANCIENT SOURCES
AND THE ANCIENT CONCEPT OF DECLINE

Despite historical inconsistencies, Gardiner made Greek sport fit his idealism and schema.[82] We should not excuse him for this but we should understand him fully as influenced by his cultural milieu and also by his classical research. Using ancient evidence selectively and prescriptively to bolster his myths, Gardiner misread his sources to find and date an ideal age of amateurism, but he did not misread his sources concerning the ancient perception of history as in decline. His predisposition to see decline was reinforced by his classicist's familiarity with that motif in ancient literature—especially in Aristophanes.

Gardiner's use of ancient literary sources is often predictable and derivative. He uses Homer, as many Hellenists did, to suggest the pure infancy of the ideal. Homer shows the early joy of effort in sport. "There was nothing artificial about his sports: they were the natural product of a warlike race, part of the daily life of the family." Later Pindar verbalizes the ideal at its height. Gardiner especially likes Pindaric *aidos*, a combination of dignity and modesty, and he emphasizes Pindar as Panhellenic and patriotic.[83] We have already seen that the demise of Pindar approximates the demise of the ideal.

On the negative side, from Gardner and Mahaffy, Gardiner uses a conventional cast of critics including Xenophanes, Euripides, Plato, and military figures such as Alexander. Gardiner feels sympathy with Xenophanes, and reveres him as a tragic warner against sixth-century signs of excess adulation and rewards for athletes. Gardiner quotes and fully agrees with the diatribe against athletes from a fragment of Euripides' *Autolycus*—the "severest indictment of professionalism" and Gardiner's most concentrated source of anti-professional ammunition. The fragment, which was influenced by Xenophanes and came to influence Galen and others, rejects the custom of honoring victors more than good and wise men; it presents the athlete as a (soon stereotypical) physical caricature.[84] Gardiner declares that Euripides and Plato regarded athletes as militarily deficient. Moderns agree that such sources must be used with caution and that they had little or no impact on ancient sport, but for Gardiner they were enlightened and relevant.[85]

Gardiner makes typical use of later authors such as Galen,[86] but his use of Philostratus is somewhat curious. He unavoidably uses Philostratus' *Gymnastikos* many times on specific points, but, ironically, he makes little schematic use of Philostratus' assertion of a decline of sport with the rise of specialized intense training. Apparently Gardiner preferred to use sources of classical fame and authority, especially those contemporary with the stage of sport discussed. Moreover, Gardiner, who taught doctors' sons, disliked Philostratus' disparagement of the medical profession, and criticized him for his lack of technical knowledge of gymnastics.[87]

Most significant here is Gardiner's distinctive use of Aristophanes, for this comic playwright was not a major Victorian source. For both the theme and the chronology of decline, Gardiner's emphasis on Aristophanes, which derives from K. J. Freeman rather than Mahaffy or Gardner, is crucial and strategic.[88] Since one of Aristophanes' main topics is education, Gardiner's view of sport as a combination of athletics and education allows him to cherish and use this source extensively.

Analysis of Gardiner's works shows that passages from Aristophanes' plays are used (cited, referred to, paraphrased or quoted, or discussed) more than seventy times. Uses are roughly of two types: "neutral"—objective philological or technical cases concerning terms or rules; and "schematic" or "substantive"—value-laden uses to substantiate the chronology and extent of decline (e.g. quotes or paraphrases of Aristophanic criticism of contemporary sport). Gardiner made early and continuing use of Aristophanes, and most of these instances (about fifty) are neutral.[89] In works from between 1903 and 1906 there are more than twenty;[90] *GASF* cites Aristophanes over thirty-five times; *AAW* still has more than ten references but by then Gardiner does it even without footnotes.[91] Apparently Gardiner became familiar with the Greek playwright in his early technical research and came to value his potential for timely social criticism.

When making neutral use of Aristophanes, Gardiner is fine for his era, but the schematic cases, where Aristophanes and decline overlap, especially in the *Clouds*, reveal mythologizing. There are about twenty such uses, some with extended discussion.[92] Aristophanes gives Gardiner more reinforcement for more of his motifs and chronology of decline than any other ancient source. Consider, for example, this passage from *GASF*, 131–32, and its clone in *AAW*, 102:

> *GASF*, 131: At the time of the Persian wars the Greeks had been a nation of athletes. At the time of the Peloponnesian wars the mass of the people were no longer athletic. Aristophanes bitterly deplores the change [citing *Clouds* 961–1023; *Frogs* 1086]. At Athens the young men had deserted the palaestra and gymnasium for the luxurious baths and the marketplace; pale-faced and narrow-chested, they had not even sufficient training to run the torch race.

> *GASF*, 132: While athletics were passing into the hands of professionals and losing their hold upon the people, the richer classes devoted themselves more and more to chariot and horse races. . . . The horsiness of the fashionable young Athenian is ridiculed by Aristophanes [citing *Clouds* passim].

> *AAW*, 102: Aristophanes sadly contrasts the pale, narrow-chested youths of his day with the men who fought at Marathon [citing *Clouds* 961–1022; *Frogs* 1086]. The wrestling-schools and gymnasia were deserted for the marketplace and the baths. The gilded youth of Athens found their sport in quail-fighting and horse-racing. They preferred to be spectators of the deeds of others rather than doers.[93]

Most sport historians have overlooked the significance of Aristophanes as a temporal or diachronic critic of sport: he gives nostalgia for the past and lamentation for the present. Most early critics merely condemn adulation for athletes as a *nomos* or traditional social custom. Aristophanes gives Gardiner the historical process of decline—a change in *nomoi*.

Overall Gardiner makes most (twice as much as of any other play) and fullest use of passages from the *Clouds*, especially lines 961–1023—the debate between representatives of the old and new education. Gardiner uses Aristophanes to set the "old days" of the ideal in the Persian War era of supposed Panhellenism. The *Clouds* offers "before and after" pictures of the products of traditional and new education—the good old days of Marathon and the sad new days of the Peloponnesian War. Gardiner points out Aristophanes' use of *aidos* and the ideal of *kaloskagathos* (a combination of beauty and goodness).[94] Positive motifs include friendly rivalry, open air education, and fitness. Negative motifs applied to Aristophanes' own day of the Peloponnesian War include pale, unathletic youths, immorality, luxury, and baths. The *Frogs* also reinforces the *Clouds* with the educational theme of the corruptive influence of Euripides and Socrates. Degenerate youths lack the musical and gymnastic training of old, says Aeschylus, who fought at Marathon; and Dionysus demonstrates this with the anecdote about the torch race: crowds laugh at the spectacle of an ill-fit youth.[95] Gardiner accepts at face value as Aristophanes' own words the image that the spirit is weak, the golden youth have withdrawn into horseracing, and the gymnasia are empty.

Gardiner's use of Aristophanes is sometimes strained or selective. He finds Aristophanes readily available on education and morality but he has to stretch to find athletic over-training and the corruptive influence of money. One problem is that, although Aristophanes' characters assert athletic decline via educational decline, they do not condemn rewards for athletes. Aristophanes mentions moral and physical decline and Gardiner himself links these with professionalism and money as symptoms and influences.[96] Perhaps most telling of Gardiner's mythologizing of and from Aristophanes is his assertion that Aristophanes would agree with the diatribe of Euripides, "his inveterate foe."[97]

An exception to Gardiner's use of comedy is Aristophanes' bawdiness. The *Clouds* uses coarse bodily metaphors that Gardiner omits even though he and Aristophanes share the use of the body as symbolic of the man. Gardiner notes *Clouds* 966 saying boys were taught to sit with crossed legs but he does not say why. He cannot deal with Aristophanes' association of gymnasia with pederasty and so he ignores it.[98] Gardiner was uncomfortable talking about what he called "tender parts" of the body.[99]

Uncritically avoiding the point of it all, Gardiner felt that Aristophanes spoke to and for him as a teacher. As conservatives, Gardiner and his version of Aristophanes shared heroes at Marathon, idealized old education, and lamented the Peloponnesian War and newfangled education.[100] Ironically, Gardiner's tragic scenario for sport (with his tragic vocabulary of excess and nemesis) rests heavily on sources that were meant to be comic (with exaggeration and the rude vocabulary of burlesque). Comic stereotypes become tragic warnings. Nevertheless, there were ancient sources asserting decline, and we must acknowledge the notion of decline in Greece as well as England.

Just as Gardiner was not the first or last Englishman to sound the theme of the decline of British sport, the idea that sport—that society—was in decline from better old days was not an Aristophanic comic innovation. The idea of nostalgia for past athletic glory, and the assertion that athletics had declined from the good old days, begin at the start of Greek literature in Homer, an author Gardiner loved. From an earlier generation of better men who had contended against legendary figures, Nestor recalls past sporting victories when he was conspicuous among heroes (*Iliad* 23.630ff.). In the *Odyssey* when Odysseus challenges the Phaeacians he adds the proviso that he would not compete with the "men of old" (8.223). It would be pointless to compete against the supermen of the old days. Aristophanes' Nestor is the old Acharnian who used to run, and his hero is Phayllus, a famous athlete but also a military leader in the glory days of the Persian War.

Clearly Aristophanes' good old days theme had literary precedents. Homer's near contemporary, Hesiod, in the Myth of the Four Ages, presents *all* of life in decline from the golden age.[101] Recent scholarship seems more open to the idea of progress in Greek thought in terms of human betterment, but J. B. Bury is still correct about the prevalence of the idea that the best age was in the past: "They dreamed of a golden age, but they generally placed it behind them. They sought it in simpler, not more complex, conditions." E. R. Dodds argues that the idea of progress was not wholly foreign to antiquity, but progress was used mainly by scientific writers concerning material progress. Most philosophers were hostile to the idea and often there was a tension between a belief in scientific or technical progress and a belief in moral regress.[102]

Gardiner was well familiar with the ancient notion of decline from a golden age in authors including Homer, Hesiod, Livy, Virgil, and the Second Sophistic; but he makes most use of the motif from Aristophanes. The themes are well-worn ones: the corruption of natural, traditional life; moral decline into luxury; and condemnations of softness, effeminacy, social disruption, the city, and indolence.[103] Steeped in the ancient classics and in Victorian negative classicism, Gardiner embraced from both eras the paradox of progress as decadence—that, while performances and crowds may progress quantitatively, as he admits, nevertheless the overall pattern is a process of qualitative decline from spirit, harmony, natural excellence, and a noble ideal. As an idealist Gardiner preferred his qualitative criteria of decline, which are subjective and related to his perspective and value system—the stuff of sport mythology more than sport history.[104]

CONCLUSION

Gardiner's mythologies came from his life, his world, and his sources. As an idealist and a moralist, Gardiner was sincere and resourceful in making his contribution to the study of antiquity. He was a selective, engaged scholar led to misrepresentations by his convictions and enthusiasm. The ages of athleticism (ca. 1860–1940), amateurism (ca. 1866–1913), and Victorian Hellenism all overlap, peak, and weaken during his lifetime. Given his personal involvement in sport, teaching, and classical studies, and given the athleticism, amateurism, and Hellenism of the era, it was perhaps inevitable that Gardiner share and perpetuate myths about ancient sport.

Pushing positive classicism on the ideal and negative classicism on decline, Gardiner eloquently said what he believed, and what he felt ancient evidence indicated, to an audience wanting to believe the same thing. Victorian themes of naturalism and decline appear even in Gardiner's minor works and in his reviews. Beyond his works on sport, his involvement with societies promoting classics and Hellenism and his editing of schoolboy texts indicate his sincere defence of classical education as relevant and practical. Gardiner became set in his ways early on and then remained somewhat isolated in Surrey and in his scholarly circle. His perception of ancient decline correlated with the decline he saw around him on so many fronts: professional athletics and scientific physical education were displacing games and sport, classical education was decreasing, and the empire and British morals and society seemed to be losing strength.

We now live in a different world: educators are suspicious of athleticism, the modern Olympics are in crisis, and anthropology has all but killed idealistic Hellenism. The history of ancient sport is being rewritten, and we find Gardiner curious. Yet, whatever we say in demythologizing sport history, we must realize that we ourselves will be demythologized by a future generation of sport historians. We will always "learn from the past," but what, why, and how we learn are influenced by our present.[105] That's how the game is played.

Appendix: Bibliography of E. Norman Gardiner (1864–1930)

1. "The Method of Deciding the Pentathlon." *Journal of Hellenic Studies* 23 (1903): 54–70 (cited as "Pentathlon").
2. "Notes on the Greek Foot Race." *JHS* 23 (1903): 261–91. ("Foot Race")
3. "Phayllus and his Record Jump." *JHS* 24 (1904): 70–80. ("Phayllus")
4. "Further Notes on the Greek Jump." *JHS* 24 (1904): 179–94. ("Jump")
5. "Wrestling. I." *JHS* 25 (1905): 14–31. ("Wrestling I")
6. "Wrestling. II." *JHS* 25 (1905): 263–93. ("Wrestling II")
7. "The Pankration and Wrestling. III." *JHS* 26 (1906): 4–22. ("Pankration")
8. "Throwing the Diskos." *JHS* 27 (1907): 1–36. ("Diskos")
9. "Throwing the Javelin." *JHS* 27 (1907): 249–73. ("Javelin")
10. *Greek Athletic Sports and Festivals. Handbooks of Archaeology and Antiquities*. London: Macmillan, 1910. Reprint ed.: Dubuque, Iowa: Brown Reprint, 1970. (*GASF*)
11. "Panathenaic Amphorae." *JHS* 32 (1912): 179–93. ("Amphorae")
12. "The Alleged Kingship of the Olympic Victor." *Annual of the British School at Athens* 22 (1916): 85–105. ("Victor")
13. "The Revival of Athletic Sculpture: Dr. R. Tait McKenzie's Work." *The International Studio* 72 (1920): 133–38. ("McKenzie")
14. With Lauri Pihkala, "The System of the Pentathlon." *JHS* 45 (1925): 132–34. ("Pihkala")
15. *Olympia. Its History and Remains*. Oxford: Clarendon Press, 1925. Reprint ed.: Washington, D.C.: McGrath Publishing Co., 1973. (*OL*)
16. H. Lee-Warner, *Extracts from Livy*. New Illustrated Edition. Revised by E. Norman Gardiner. Oxford: Clarendon Press, 1927. (*Livy*)
17. *Selections from Virgil's Eclogues and Georgics*. Edited by E. Norman Gardiner. Oxford: Clarendon Press, [1928] 1930. (*Virgil*)
18. "Regulations for a Local Sports Meeting." *Classical Review* 43 (1929): 210–12. ("Regulations")
19. *Athletics of the Ancient World*. Oxford: Clarendon Press, 1930. Reprint eds.: Oxford: Clarendon Press, 1955; 1965; 1967; 1971; Chicago: Ares, 1979. (*AAW*)
20. "A School in Ptolemaic Egypt." *Classical Review* 44 (1930): 211–13. ("School")

Reviews by Gardiner:

"Greek Athletics." By F. A. Wright. *JHS* 45 (1925): 145–46. ("Wright")

"Der Sport im Altertum." By Bruno Schröder. *JHS* 48 (1928): 125–26. ("Schröder")

"Körperkultur im Altertum." By Julius J. Jüthner. *JHS* 48 (1928): 252. ("Jüthner")

"Greek Physical Culture." By Clarence Forbes. *JHS* 50 (1930): 350. ("Forbes")

"La Danse Grecque." By Louis Séchan. *JHS* 50 (1930): 350–51. ("Séchan")

NOTES

1. See W. H. McNeill, *Mythistory and Other Essays* (Chicago: University of Chicago, 1986), including his "Mythistory, or Truth, Myth, History and Historians," *American Historical Review* 91 no. 1 (1986): 1–10, on how historians influence and are influenced by their culture. Similarly, but with reference to ancient history, M. I. Finley, *Ancient History: Evidence and Models* (New York: Viking Penguin, 1986), explains that all historians use conceptual schemes or simplifying assumptions to make sense of the complexities of human history.

2. See F. J. Frost, "The Dubious Origins of the 'Marathon'," *American Journal of Ancient History* 4 (1979): 159–63. Other examples: the ancient Olympic truce did not establish a "total and binding truce" throughout Greece: see M. Lämmer, "The Nature and Function of the Olympic Truce in Ancient Greece," in Y. Imamura et al., eds., *History of Physical Education and Sport*, vol. 3 (1975–76) (Tokyo: Kodancha, 1977), 37–52; and the five Olympic rings are not an ancient symbol: see David C. Young, "The Riddle of the Rings," in Susan J. Bandy, ed., *Coroebus Triumphs* (San Diego: San Diego State University, 1988), 257–76.

3. The status of sport studies until recently has delayed major works on obvious topics like the Roman circus. Jean-Paul Thuillier, "Les Cirques Romains," *Échos du Monde Classique/Classical Views* 31 n.s. 6 (1987): 93–94, refers to "un certain blocage intellectuel" causing a preference for studies of religious over sporting architecture. It is ironic that two of the most provocative studies of the last decade have come from classicists who happened upon sport history. Cf. David C. Young, *The Olympic Myth of Greek Amateur Athletics* (Chicago: Ares, 1984), vii–viii; and David Sansone, *Greek Athletics and the Genesis of Sport* (Berkeley, Los Angeles and London: University of California, 1988), xiii–xiv.

4. E.g. John M. Hoberman, *Sport and Political Ideology* (Austin: University of Texas Press, 1984), discusses major twentieth-century European sport ideologies as expressions of political doctrine.

5. Cf. Norbert Elias and Eric Dunning, *Quest for Excitement: Sport and Leisure in the Civilizing Process* (Oxford: Basil Blackwell, 1986).

6. H. W. Pleket, "Games, Prizes, Athletes and Ideology. Some Aspects of the History of Sport in the Greco-Roman World," *Stadion* 1 (1975): 51.

7. For Gardiner's bibliography and abbreviations used herein, see the appendix. The *Oxford Classical Dictionary*, 2nd ed., cites him on "Olympics," "Olympian Games,"

and "Athletics." *Der Kleine Pauly, Lexicon der Antike*, 1964–75, 5 vols., vol. 1 (1964): 140, recommends *GASF* and *AAW* on "agon(es)"; vol. 4 (1972): 283, recommends *OL* on "Olympia." *The Encyclopaedia Britannica Macropaedia*, vol. 25 (1986): 201, recommends *GASF* and *AAW* on "Olympic Games."

8. *AAW*, "Preface to the American Edition," v. In *Greek and Roman Athletics: A Bibliography* (Chicago: Ares, 1984), 17, Thomas F. Scanlon says Gardiner "remains the most distinguished and lucid English writer·on Greek athletics. . . . [*GASF* is] still the single most useful English book on that topic." Grant L. Dunlop, in an introduction (no page numbers) for Brown Reprints to the 1970 reprint of *GASF*, says, "His treatment of the subject was so exhaustive, his scholarship so thorough, that other writers in the field could only stand back in awe."

9. See his *Myth*, especially chap. 6, "E. N. Gardiner, James Thorpe, and Avery Brundage," 76–88. Cf. my review in *Échos du Monde Classique/Classical Views* 29 n.s. 4 (1985): 134–42.

10. I would like to acknowledge the assistance of Mrs. Christine Butler, assistant archivist, Corpus Christi College, Oxford; Drs. D. J. Geagan, Douglas M. Swallow, and Gary D. Stark; and the library staffs of the University of Texas at Arlington and McMaster University. Normal biographical reference sources, such as the *Dictionary of National Biography*, simply ignore Gardiner, but see *The (London) Times* Oct. 21, 1930, p. 19, col. 3; *The Pelican Record* 20 no. 1 (1930) 16–17; *Classical Review* 44 no. 6 (Dec., 1930), 209–10, "Notes and News"; and Joseph Foster, *Alumni Oxonienses: Members of the University of Oxford, 1715–1888* (Oxford and London: Parker and Co., 1888), vol. 1–2, 507.

11. The former dates seem to be in error: Gardiner probably played rugby for Devonshire while a master at Newton College for three years after Oxford (1887–90), with his play for the Western Counties (1888–89) as the highlight of his career.

12. See appendix. George A. Macmillan, *A History of the Hellenic Society* (London: Society for the Promotion of Hellenic Studies, 1929), xxxiii, under "Publications" takes special notice of the significance of Gardiner's contributions to *JHS* along with those of W. W. Tarn and J. D. Beazley. Gardiner also attended and participated in annual general meetings of the Society: Macmillan, *Hellenic Society*, xliii, xlviii; "Victor," 85.

13. *JHS* 51 (1931): xx, xxv.

14. Macmillan, *Hellenic Society*, xxxiv–xxxvi, xxxix.

15. *Classical Review* 40 nos. 1–2 (Feb.–Mar. 1926) through 44 no. 5 (Nov., 1930).

16. *The (London) Times* Jan. 15, 1931, p. 8, col. 6.

17. *CR* 44 no. 6 (Dec. 1930): 209–10.

18. *GASF*, Preface, viii: "The attempt [to write a full history of Greek athletics] is an ambitious one, perhaps too ambitious for one whose occupation has left him little time for continuous study."

19. "Pentathlon" is an examination of various hypotheses concerning the method of deciding victory in the pentathlon. Gardiner returned to the issue in *JHS* in 1925 with a brief piece agreeing with Pihkala's suggestion on the pentathlon and supporting the idea of applying this newly discovered (but unprovable) ancient system of "comparative victories" to the modern Olympics. "Phayllus" rejects the Greek epigram about Phayllus' fifty-five-foot jump as an exaggerated tall tale. "Jump" argues that the Greeks used only a long jump and a standing jump. "Foot Race," "Wrestling I," "Wrestling II," "Pankration," "Diskos," and "Javelin" all discuss evidence, techniques, rules, terminology, and any relevant equipment. Almost all of this material ended up in *GASF*.

20. E.g.: "Pentathlon," 54; 56: "To anyone who has the least acquaintance with athletics, this is so obvious as scarcely to need restating. . . ."; 59: "This ingenious theory

smacks of the midnight oil but surely not of the oil of the palaestra." Gardiner also was skeptical of the value of the ancient Scholiasts for their bookishness and lack of practical experience: "Pentathlon," 64; "Jump," 73; "Diskos," 3–4.

21. "Pankration," 5, 12, says this was a contest of skill not strength before it became brutal with professionalism and specialization—a notion rejected by M. B. Poliakoff, "Melankomas EK KLIMAKOS and Greek Boxing," *American Journal of Philology* 108 no. 3 (1987): 511–18.

22. *GASF,* viii: "The place of physical training and games in education, the place of athletics in our daily life and in our national life, are questions of present importance to us all, and in considering these questions we cannot fail to learn something from the athletic history of a nation which for a time at least succeeded in reconciling the rival claims of body and mind, and immortalizing this result in its art."

23. Own judgements: *GASF,* viii, *OL,* viii. *GASF,* ix: "Further, I have endeavoured clearly to distinguish between what is certain and what is conjectural." Gardiner could be appropriately incredulous about some information, e.g. "Phayllus," 79: "Now no records are so liable to exaggeration as athletic records, especially when based not on written evidence but on report and tradition."

24. "Amphorae," 190. Cf. my *Athletics in Ancient Athens* (Leiden: Brill, 1987), 176–77.

25. "Victor," 85, 87; *OL,* chap. 5, "The Origin of the Olympic Festival," 58–76.

26. *AAW,* xiv: "I have also included illustrations of the athletic bronzes of my friend, Dr. R. Tait McKenzie. They are the nearest modern parallel to the athletic art of Greece." Also see "Wright," 145–46.

27. Reviewing *OL,* R. M. Dawkins, *JHS* 46 (1926): 134, declares it "eminently satisfactory." W. W. Hyde, *AJPhil.* 48 (1927): 186–91, calls it "an authoritative presentation of all that is known about ancient Olympia and its famous games." Decline: e.g.: *OL,* 66, says the development of hero worship in the sixth century produced "excesses"; honors became extravagant with the "decline of sport and the growth of luxury."

28. *Livy,* Preface, v.

29. H. Lister's book notice in *CR* 42 (1928): 68, says: "This is in every way a delightful book. . . . If we must have selections, let us have them like this."

30. In his "Life of Virgil," 20, Gardiner cannot resist elaborating on a minor sporting point: Virgil's health prevents him from joining Maecenas at ball games. Gardiner, 24, 106, 109, applauds Virgil as a "practical bee-keeper" with "personal experience."

31. *Virgil,* 25, 81. Gardiner, 113–15, cannot escape religion concerning the 4th "Messianic" Eclogue: he is open to the idea that Virgil got his Messianic ideas indirectly from the East and from Isaiah; he reveres both Virgil and Isaiah as "great seers."

32. *AAW,* xiii. Reviewing *AAW* in *JHS* 51 (1931): 305, H. Mattingly says ". . . the special value of the book lies in its expert presentation and interpretation of the abundant evidence, literary and monumental. Gardiner was a classical scholar with much personal experience and wide interest in athletics."

33. "Regulations," 211.

34. Cf. *AAW,* 116, addendum. "Notes and News," *CR* 44 no. 6 (Dec., 1930): 210, comments on the article: ". . . it [along with the article of 1929] illustrates the wide range of his reading, his alertness in the search for evidence, and the sobriety of his judgement."

35. "School," 211–12. Gardiner's personality, sometimes but not always humble, came out in reviews. In 1925 he is rather condescending to Wright's "somewhat inaccurate little book": he criticizes both Wright and Schröder (in 1928) for supporting scientific physical culture. He charges Schröder with inaccuracy, misinterpretations of vases, and

"little practical knowledge of athletics." By contrast, his 1928 review of Jüthner praises him as "master of his subject." Finally, *JHS* 50 Part II of 1930 (issued Jan. 30, 1931), 350, contains two posthumous reviews by Gardiner, one critical of Forbes for incompleteness and "the artificial separation of athletics and gymnastics," and one praising Séchan's as "a truly fascinating book" on the details and spirit of Greek dance, with chapters on the reform of modern dance.

36. See *GASF*, 8–11; *OL*, 17–18, 34; *AAW*, 1, 14. Such ideas of Greek exclusiveness, advanced by J. Burckhardt and others, have now been challenged. Agonism was not uniquely or aboriginally Greek, yet, as Michael B. Poliakoff, *Combat Sports in the Ancient World* (New Haven and London: Yale University Press, 1987), 104–15, notes, the Greeks were distinctive in the number and nature of their competitions and in their institutionalization of rewards and recognition for victors.

37. See *GASF*, chap. 2, "Athletics in Homer," especially 11–26; chap. 3, "The Rise of the Athletic Festival," 27–61; chap. 4, "The Age of Athletic Festivals, Sixth Century B.C.," 62–85. *GASF*, 60–62; *AAW*, 42: "Athletics were in sympathy with the growing spirit of democracy. . . . At the close of the sixth century the Greeks were literally a nation of athletes."

38. *GASF*, 101; see chap. 5, "The Age of the Athletic Ideal, 500–440 B.C.," 86–121; 2–4.

39. *AAW*, 100. In *GASF*, 184, Gardiner agrees with K. J. Freeman that Spartan education was the prototype of the English schoolboy system. "Foot Race," 261, and "Pentathlon," n. 39 on p. 62 parallel Greek athletic meets with those of British schools.

40. *GASF*, 61, 1, 107–108; *AAW*, 93, 42: "The victory of Greeks over Persians was the victory of free states over oriental despotism; it was the victory of a handful of trained athletes over hordes of effeminate barbarians."

41. *GASF*, 130. Signs of problems appeared in the sixth century with a change in athletic attitudes to a more one-sided ideal: *GASF*, 78–79, 122. See also chap. 6, "Professionalism and Specialization, 440–338 B.C.," 122–45; *AAW*, chap. 8, "Professionalism," 99–116.

42. *AAW*, 3, 101; *GASF*, 5–6.

43. *AAW*, 104, 44. See also *GASF*, 82, 131–32, and chap. 7, "The Decline of Greek Athletics, 338–146 B.C.," 146–72.

44. Cf. *GASF*, 2, 135. David C. Young's assertion in "How the Amateurs Won the Olympics," in Wendy J. Raschke, ed., *The Archaeology of the Olympics* (Madison: University of Wisconsin Press, 1988), 71, that "evil" is "a word appearing on almost every other page in Gardiner's books" is an overstatement, but "evil" was a well-worn and favorite word in Gardiner's moralizing: e.g. inter alia: *GASF*, 79; *OL*, 97, 134, 149; *AAW*, 100, 104–105.

45. *GASF*, 122. "Excess" is Gardiner's word for hubris or insolence, the opposite of *aidos* or modesty. Cf. inter alia *GASF*, 79, 82, 112; *OL*, 66, 106; *AAW*, 99. The nemesis line appeared early and persisted: "Phayllus," 71; *AAW*, 99.

46. Cf. Richard Haywood, *The Myth of Rome's Fall* (New York: Crowell, 1958). For cautions about notions of monolithic and monocausal decline, and for a treatment of the problem of quantifying decline, see Ramsay MacMullen, *Corruption and the Decline of Rome* (New Haven and London: Yale University Press, 1988), 1–15.

47. Scanlon, *Bibliography*, 17: "It can no longer be assumed that there was a 'rise and fall' of Greek athletics which accompanied fifth century cultural progress. . . ." Scanlon's "The Ecumenical Olympics: The Games in the Roman Era," in Jeffrey O. Segrave and Donald Chu, eds., *The Olympic Games in Transition* (Champaign, Ill.: Hu-

man Kinetics Books, 1988), 37–64, shows that the games became transformed in the wider Roman world.

48. "Wrestling I," 14; *GASF,* 79, 136; *OL,* 148; *AAW,* 44, 99, 102.

49. *GASF,* 2, 4, chap. 5, "The Age of the Athletic Ideal, 500–440 B.C.," 86–121; *OL,* 106; *AAW,* 42–43, 53, 64.

50. *GASF,* 122, 131, 135: "The struggle between Athens and Sparta . . . contributed in no small degree to the decay of athletics."

51. J. A. Mangan, *Athleticism and the Victorian and Edwardian Public School. The Emergence and Consolidation of an Educational Ideology* (Cambridge: Cambridge University Press, 1981), 9. Mangan explains (p. 2) that public schools were "for the well-to-do, expensive, predominantly boarding, independent of the state, but neither privately owned nor profit-making."

52. Ibid., 28–42, 135–38.

53. Ibid., 182–86, 199, 205–206. Mangan comments (p. 6) that athleticism" embraced a complex of ideas and feelings deliberately and carefully created through ritual and symbol; that it was, on occasion, a form of 'pseudo-reasoning,' a deliberate rationalization for ambitions such as status and power; and that it constituted value-judgements masquerading as facts to reinforce commitment."

54. Ibid., 22–28, 88, 208.

55. Brian Gardner, *The Public Schools. An Historical Survey* (London: Hamish Hamilton Ltd., 1973), 177.

56. Mangan, *Athleticism,* 126.

57. *GASF,* 4, 124, 187: "Both health-culture and professionalism are poles removed from the true Greek ideal of athletics." Also see *AAW,* 1–2; "Wright," 145; "Schröder," 125; and "Forbes," 350.

58. *GASF,* 107.

59. *AAW,* 98. Cf. Mangan, *Athleticism,* 198–200.

60. Young, *Myth,* 78, 80–82. Young sees three elements in Gardiner's amateur ideology: 1) social elitism was the main issue, 2) money in sport is always evil, and 3) being too good in sports by excessive training is bad. Also see his "Professionalism in Archaic and Classical Greek Athletics," *Ancient World* 7 nos. 1–2 (1983): 45–51; and his "How the Amateurs Won the Olympics," in Raschke, *Archaeology,* 55–75.

61. Young, *Myth,* 51–53: "Although Mahaffy founded the myth of ancient amateurism, he never idealized the Greeks. . . . it was Percy Gardner who inspired E. N. Gardiner, the source of all our gross misconceptions about our subject."

62. Gardiner does not refer to Mahaffy's "Old Greek Athletics," *Macmillan's Magazine* 36 (1879): 61–69, the piece that influenced P. Gardner—cf. 272 of Gardner's "Olympia and the Festival," chap. 9, 265–304, of his *New Chapters in Greek History* (London: John Murray, 1892). However, Gardiner in "Foot Race," 267 n. 33 and 269 n. 37, cites p. 310 of Mahaffy's *Rambles and Studies in Greece,* 3rd ed., (London: Macmillan and Co., 1887): 275–95, which, aside from an introductory paragraph, is a verbatim republication of "Old Greek Athletics."

63. Young, *Myth,* 53–56. *GASF,* xi; Young, *Myth,* n. 47 on p. 52. Fifteen years later Gardiner acknowledged Gardner again in the preface to *OL,* viii.

64. Gardner contributed many Hellenist ideas to Gardiner about nudity, art, climate, decline, and more; cf. Gardner's *New Chapters,* 269–70, 271, 274, 299, 301.

65. *AAW,* 105. Gardiner denounces the "evil" results of professionalism as "fatal to the true amateur spirit" and charges that "when money enters into sport, corruption is sure to follow." See *GASF,* 134; *AAW,* 3, 103.

66. As Young notes, in Raschke, *Archaeology*, 70: "The true author of amateurism was the British public school."

67. In *OL*, 67, and "Victor," 96, Gardiner rejects as a "hasty and inaccurate gener-alization" Gardner's notion, "Olympia," 299, that part of the victor's city's wall was torn down for his triumphal return. Young, *Myth*, n. 49 on p. 54: "Even E. N. Gardiner would not be taken in with that error." *AAW*'s selected bibliography lacks Gardner and Mahaffy and has more references to J. Jüthner than to anyone else—except to Gardiner himself. Gardiner also expressed debts to superior British scholars, as to J. D. Beazley in *AAW*, xiv.

68. Young, *Myth*, 15–27, shows that the age of amateurism (1866–1913) actually postdates professional sport. For an economic history of the emergence of British profes-sional sport, see Wray Vamplew, *Pay Up and Play the Game. Professional Sport in Brit-ain 1875–1914* (Cambridge: Cambridge University Press, 1988).

69. *GASF*, 10; noted by Young, *Myth*, 76.

70. William J. Baker, *Sports in the Western World* (Totowa, N.J.: Rowan and Littlefield, 1982), 119–37. Young, *Myth*, n. 72 on pp. 76–77, notes Gardiner's analogy (*GASF*, n. 2 on p. 131; *AAW*, 50) of later Greek athletics to the use of hired football pro-fessionals from the country districts of Scotland to represent English towns.

71. E.g.: "Diskos," 7, 10–11.

72. *GASF*, 6–7, 1, 5.

73. John Kieran, Arthur Daley, and Pat Jordan, *The Story of the Olympic Games: 776 B.C. to 1976* (Philadelphia and New York: J. B. Lippincott, 1977), 63. *New York Times*, July 29, 1908, p. 9; noted in George R. Matthews, "The Controversial Olympic Games of 1908 as Viewed by the New York Times and The Times of London," *Journal of Sport History* 7 no. 2 (1980): 50.

74. See Frank M. Turner, *The Greek Heritage in Victorian Britain* (New Haven and London: Yale University Press, 1981); Richard Jenkyns, *The Victorians and Ancient Greece* (Oxford: Basil Blackwell, 1980); and David Lowenthal, *The Past is a Foreign Country* (Cambridge: Cambridge University Press, 1985), 96–105. Arnoldo Momigli-ano, "Declines and Fall," *American Scholar* 49 no. 1 (Winter 1979–80), 40, contrasts the relative optimism of Gibbon and the eighteenth century with the atmosphere of the 1880s, "when the problem of decadence in its general terms had developed out of the roots of the social crisis of contemporary Europe."

75. Turner, *Greek Heritage*, 4–8, 16, 82, 447.

76. Ibid., "The Hellenism of Matthew Arnold," 17–36. Jenkyns, *The Victorians*, 60–62, 69, 73–77. Cf. Warren D. Anderson, *Matthew Arnold and the Classical Tradi-tion* (Ann Arbor: University of Michigan Press, 1965).

77. Turner, *Greek Heritage*, 39–42. Jenkyns, *The Victorians*, 44–45, 133–34, 195, 225.

78. His idealism began early: "Pentathlon," 54: "The sense of Fairness and Order was characteristic of the Greek mind. . . ."

79. *AAW*, 57; Jenkyns, *The Victorians*, 219–25; 248. E.g. W. W. Capes, Reader in Ancient History at Oxford, *University Life in Ancient Athens*, an 1877 publication of four Oxford lectures, reprint ed., (New York: G. E. Stechert and Co., 1922), 4–28, turns the Greek *ephebeia* (the institutionalized military training of young men) into a British school by discussing academic dress and final exams.

80. Patrick Brantlinger, *Bread and Circuses: Theories of Mass Culture and Social Decay* (Ithaca and London: Cornell University, 1983), 9–12, 18, 31–32, 45, 50. Negative classicism interprets mass culture as a symptom or cause of social decay, often comparing

modern society with the Roman imperial decadence of "bread and circuses"—the classical form of mass culture. This is a catastrophic or cyclical view of history rather than a progressive one. Brantlinger focuses on modern mass culture and the cultural effects of democratization, industrialism, and mass media, but he also notes classical roots for the myth; cf. 53–81.

81. Ibid., 185. Brantlinger could well be describing Gardiner when he says that modern conservatives, such as Ortega, Eliot, and Camus, fear mass culture as "commercial rather than free or unconditioned, plebian or bourgeois and vulgar rather than aristocratic and 'noble,' based on self-interest rather than on high ideals . . . urban . . . rather than close to nature."

82. The individual nature of Greek athletic competition, the absence in the crown games of team events, might have been a problem for Gardiner, but he escaped by turning the ideal athlete into a citizen-soldier who conformed to the collectivity of his *polis*.

83. *GASF*, 13. Turner, *Greek Heritage*, 135–37, 171–73, and Jenkyns, *The Victorians*, 210–26, note that Victorians felt Homer expressed Greek ideals of the classical age analogous to those of Britain. *GASF*, 102–106, 109–12, applauds Pindar's moralism and his concept of *kaloskagathos*, the combination of beauty and goodness: Pindar shows the Greek educational aim of harmonious development of mind and body. Earlier, "Pankration," n. 36 on p. 13, gave features of Pindar's ideal: "strength, beauty, training, skill, courage, endurance."

84. *GASF*, 122, 131; *AAW*, 103. *GASF*, 5, 79: while Xenophanes showed signs of excess, Euripides, for Gardiner, shows the results of corruption. (Cf. Gardner, *New Chapters*, 302, who is cautious about the fragment: "Perhaps in the strictures of this poet we may see too much of the sophist. . . .") Nevertheless, Gardiner embraces Euripides as a former victor appreciative of all manly sports: *GASF*, 131–32. *AAW*, 103, extensively quotes the fragment.

85. *GASF*, 127–29; cf. Gardner, *New Chapters*, 300–301. See Jenkyns, *The Victorians*, 227–61, on Victorian use of Plato as a moralist and social critic advocating social duty against the trend to a pluralistic society. On Euripides and other critics as unreliable and ineffectual, see Kyle, *Athens*, 124–41.

86. E.g. "Pankration," 13: Galen and medical writers condemn the evil effects of "the utterly unscientific system of training introduced by professionalism, a life of overfeeding, over-sleeping, over-exercise. . . ." *GASF*, 186–87: Galen has "breadth of mind and fearless love of truth."

87. Uses of Philostratus: e.g. *OL*, 166; *GASF*, 174, 186–89; *AAW*, 55, 115–17. Criticisms of Philostratus: *GASF* 189–92, 287 n. 1; "Pankration," 12. Poliakoff, *Combat Sports*, 4, urges caution about notions of a golden age of sport in authors of the Second Sophistic, such as Plutarch, Lucian, and Philostratus, who "have a tendency to take a nostalgic trip down memory lane."

88. Jenkyns, *The Victorians*, 79: ". . . of all the great Greek writers Aristophanes had the least influence in the last century. The Victorians did not greatly value the comic muse, and in any case teachers shrank from introducing their pupils to so rich a storehouse of obscenity." Neither Gardner nor Mahaffy used Aristophanes in their articles on Greek sport. Cf. K. J. Freeman, *Schools of Hellas; An Essay on the Practice and Theory of Ancient Greek Education from 600 to 300 B.C.*, ed. M. J. Rendall, (London: Macmillan, orig. publ. 1907; reprint ed. Port Washington, N.Y.: Kennikat Press, 1969), who made considerable use of Aristophanes, 123–36, including the *Clouds* and *Frogs* on the history of sport. As a Hellenist, Freeman speaks, 3–5, of the "spirit of Hellas" and the "ideals" of Hellenic education; he seeks the "lesson" of Hellenic schools for the modern

world. P. 287: Greeks had "a reasonable horror of undue specialization at school." Gardiner used Freeman's book in "Javelin," 267, when it appeared in 1907, and it turns up in the *GASF* bibliography. *GASF* and Freeman had the same publisher and Gardiner even used some of Freeman's illustrations and line drawings.

89. Neutral uses (several are repetitions as material moves from *JHS* to *GASF* to *AAW*): *Knights* ll. 261–63: "Wrestling II," n. 34 on 272, 291–92; *GASF*, 399–400; ll. 272–73: *GASF*, n. 1 on 446; *AAW*, n. 1 on 215; l. 387: "Wrestling II," n. 60 on 280; l. 454: *GASF*, n. 1 on 446; *AAW*, n. 1 on 215; l. 491: "Wrestling II," 272; *GASF*, 386; *AAW*, 189; l. 496: "Wrestling II," n. 34 on 272; l. 571: *GASF*, n. 4 on 377; ll. 1159–62: "Foot Race," 264, *GASF*, n. 5 on 273; n. 1 on 276; n. 6 on 277; *AAW*, n. 2 on 136; l. 1238: *GASF*, n. 2 on 503. *Birds* l. 141: *GASF*, n. 2 on 468; l. 291: "Foot Race," 281; *GASF*, n. 2 on 287, 291; l. 442ff.: "Pankration," 5–6; *GASF*, n. 2 on 374; *GASF*, 438; *AAW*, 212. *Acharnians* l. 213: "Phayllus," 77, 78; *GASF*, 309; *AAW*, 152; l. 481: "Foot Race," n. 22 on 264; l. 571: "Wrestling II," n. 60 on 280. *Peace* l. 880: *GASF*, 217; l. 895: *GASF*, n. 2 on 374, n. 2 on 448; l. 899: "Pankration," 5; *GASF*, n. 2 on 448; *AAW*, 212. *Lysistrata* l. 82: *GASF*, 296; l. 1000: "Foot Race," 263; *GASF*, 277; l. 1002: "Foot Race," 290; *GASF*, 292–93. *Clouds* l. 522: "Wrestling II," 293; l. 966: *AAW*, 90; l. 973: *GASF*, n. 2 on 503. *Wasps* l. 1203 (sic) should be 1206: "Phayllos" 77; l. 1203: "Foot Race," 290; *GASF*, 293. *Frogs* l. 710: *GASF* n. 1 on 481; l. 904: *GASF* n. 5 on 376. *Wealth* l. 1129: *GASF*, n. 4 on 296. *Ecclesiazusae* l. 1090: "Wrestling II," 280. Unspecified general reference on oriental cults: *OL*, 124.

90. "Footrace," 290, has several citations of Aristophanes, including use of the *Frogs* on the deplorable runner in the Kerameikos and on the "degenerate youth of Aristophanes' day"; 262 refers to the later decline of running "with the growth of professionalism and luxury." "Phayllus," 77, takes Aristophanes' old days as ca. the Persian War. In "Wrestling I," "Wrestling II," and "Pankration," Aristophanes is mainly used neutrally, with Philostratus and Galen brought in to show decline in later centuries. "Pentathlon," "Jump," "Diskos," and "Javelin" all lack both Aristophanes and the theme of decline.

91. E.g. *AAW*, 152: no footnote for an obvious use of *Acharnians* 213.

92. Schematic use of Aristophanes begins in "Foot Race"; see note 90 above. By *GASF* the schema is strong with a half-dozen schematic uses of the *Clouds* (esp. 961ff.): *GASF* adds diachronic to the earlier mainly technical use of Aristophanes. *GASF*, chap. 6, has five schematic uses, with three of these repeated in *AAW*, chap. 7. Schematic uses: *Clouds* passim: *GASF*, 132; l. 835: *GASF*, 479; ll. 961–1023: "Amphorae," 187: *GASF*, 106, 131; *AAW*, 102; l. 991: *GASF*, 479; ll. 995ff.: *GASF*, n. 1 on 103; l. 1005: *GASF*, 472; l. 1008: *AAW*, 84; l. 1045: *GASF*, 479. *Frogs* ll. 1086–87: "Foot Race," 290; *GASF*, 131, 292–93; *AAW*, 102; l. 1089ff.: "Foot Race," 290; *AAW*, 143. *Wealth* l. 1161: *GASF*, 129, *AAW*, 102. *Knights* l. 571: "Wrestling I," 21; l. 1060: *GASF*, 479. *Peace* ll. 33–34: *GASF*, n. 1 on 127.

93. Gardiner here also condemns the influence of money on sport and cites *Wealth* 1161.

94. *GASF*, 103, first use of *Clouds* 995ff. on *aidos*.

95. Also, "Wrestling I," 21–22, makes schematic use of *Knights* 571 on the "dogged tenacity of the men of the older generation who had made Athens great. . . . The point is that these old Athenians, however clearly they were thrown, would never admit a defeat, but would wipe off the dust and go on wrestling, as though they had not been thrown at all." Where we now would see immorality or "winning above all," Gardiner saw a military metaphor, probably for the triumph at Salamis after the sack of Athens.

96. From *Peace* 33ff., the metaphor of falling on food "like a wrestler" is used by Gardiner to suggest the gluttony of overdeveloped athletes. It probably just analogizes a beetle's movements to wrestling holds. Gardiner uses *Wealth* 1161f. on the fondness of Plutus for games to assert the excessiveness of prizes, but this may simply refer to embezzlement. Cf. Aristophanes' criticisms of the number of Athenian festivals: *Knights* 528, 1037; *Peace* 1036. Followers of Gardiner continued to misuse Aristophanes: e.g. C. Manning, "Professionalism in Greek Athletics," *Classical World* 11 (1917): 76–77; Thomas Woody, "Professionalism and the Decay of Greek Athletics," *School and Society* 47 (1938): 521–24.

97. *GASF*, 132.

98. *AAW*, 90. Pederasty and gymnasia: *Knights* 1385, 1387; *Clouds* 417, 991; *Peace* 762–63; *Wasps* 1025. Cf. K. J. Dover, *Greek Homosexuality* (Cambridge, Mass.: Harvard University Press, 1978), 40, 54–55, 138. Victorians excused license in Aristophanes and others in various ways; as Jenkyns, *The Victorians*, 281, says: "Greek smut is clean smut."

99. E.g. "Pankration," 5; "Meeting," 210.

100. J. P. Mahaffy, *Old Greek Education* (London: Kegan Paul, Trench and Co., 1881), 40–41, uses the *Clouds* but cautions that Aristophanes is exaggerating a traditional theme of the "good old days" and contemporary degeneracy. K. J. Dover, *Aristophanic Comedy* (Berkeley and Los Angeles: University of California Press, 1972), 114, calls Aristophanes' remarks about degenerate youth "a vivid comic caricature of familiar constant."

101. *Virgil*, 114: Gardiner was familiar with Hesiod's metaphorical presentation of widespread social decline, an idea probably deriving from the Near East and persisting in the Greek mind.

102. J. B. Bury, *Ancient Historians* (New York: Dover Publications, 1958; orig. publ. 1908), 205. In his *The Idea of Progress* (New York: Dover Publications, 1960; orig. publ. 1930), he sees the notion of indefinite progress as a comparatively recent idea absent in antiquity. E. R. Dodds, "The Ancient Concept of Progress," 1–25, in his *The Ancient Concept of Progress and Other Essays on Greek Literature and Belief* (Oxford: Clarendon Press, 1973).

103. Such motifs intrude even in Gardiner's *Livy*, introduction, 1: Samnites degenerate when they settle down in cities in Capua; 13: contrasts healthy northern Italy with "Rome with its luxury and vice."

104. In a perhaps telling note, Gardiner may be doing some soul-searching late in his career: *Virgil*, 90: "Compare the Gospel of Labour [Georgic 1.118–46] with the picture of the Golden Age in Eclogue 4, or the account of the Fall in Genesis. Poets of all ages have dreamt of a Golden Age, of an ideal state of nature. Did it ever exist? Can it ever exist? Is there more happiness in an unprogressive Golden Age than in a progressive civilization? How did evil come into the world, was it a punishment for sin, or that man might learn to conquer it?"

105. Lowenthal, *The Past*, shows that in trying to understand or preserve the past we inevitably alter it via human attitudes such as nostalgia and modernism. Pp. xvi–xvii, xxv: "The past is a foreign country whose features are shaped by today's predilections. . . . And as we remake it, the past remakes us."

STEPHEN HARDY

Entrepreneurs, Structures, and the Sportgeist: Old Tensions in a Modern Industry

FOR SOME TIME, historians have pondered the origins of sports, those cultural phenomena typically defined by phrases such as "institutionalized game forms," and "competitive activities" that require "physical skill," and have "play-like" or "nonutilitarian" aspects. In the effort to understand the sports booms of the last century or so, scholars have sometimes groped through the darker recesses of evidence about ancient and medieval pastimes, looking for linkages between the sports of different epochs.

This approach has been jolted in the last dozen years by the work of Allen Guttmann and Richard Mandell. They have argued forcefully that sports as we know them are something new under the sun. As Mandell notes in his *Sport: A Cultural History*, "it is idle to look for the precursors of the competitions and games of modern industrial society by tracing the history of these activities themselves." Doubtless Mandell would question the work of Robert W. Henderson, who traced the evolution of baseball back to an Egyptian ritual of throwing objects symbolizing the head of Osiris! While Mandell is willing to accept the notion of some "persistent and perhaps constant" elements in "human nature or in society" that form the basis for sport, he joins Guttmann, Melvin Adelman and others of the "modernization" school in emphasizing the *differences* between our sports and those of ancient, folk, or medieval cultures. Specifically, these differences lie in the growth of bureaucracies, the focus on records and quantifiable performance, increased specialization of roles, increased equality in and for competition, and the move to standardized rules and techniques.[1]

In a recent, provocative book, David Sansone disagrees with Mandell, Guttmann, and the modernists. Sansone believes he has found an essential feature that explains the origins and persistent patterns of behavior for all sports and yet allows for the diversity of activities that may be considered sport. According to Sansone, the origin and persistent essence of any sport relates to its function as "*the ritual sacrifice of human energy* [emphasis added]." Drawing from the work of Karl Meuli and Walter Burkert, with evidence pieced together from ancient and ethnographical sources, Sansone traces the origins of sport back to the rituals of primitive hunting tribes, who "after killing and eating [their] prey, sought by ritual means to revivify the slain animal" through such practices as stuffing the skin of the victim. These and similar rituals lessened anxieties about the availability of future prey.[2]

Even after paleolithic times, such respect toward the "game" continued in the form of blood sacrifices and libations. In Sansone's words, "even in a period of dependence upon agriculture and domesticated animals, the ancient Greeks and many other peoples engaged in ritual sacrifices that included all the elements of the rituals the hunters had developed." But one thing was missing from the earlier hunting days. This was the "conspicuous expenditure of energy"—the hunt itself—which was part of the exchange with nature, the giving *of* something *for* something. Libations and blood sacrifices would only go so far. Something had to replace the actual energy expenditure that had been essential to the hunt.[3]

As Sansone says, "it is characteristic of humans that patterns of behavior do not simply die out. The element that is absent from the blood sacrifice persisted and was itself ritualized. It became sport, which is itself a form of sacrifice." Hunting and fishing are direct descendants of the tribal activities, but so too were the forerunners of most modern sports. They were nothing more than "expenditure, waste, squandering" in new attire. These forerunners, exemplified in the great athletic festivals of ancient Greece, included a logic that Sansone believes defined a person's status: "he who can run the fastest or throw the farthest or lift the most has the greatest amount of energy to sacrifice, and is therefore worthy of the greatest honor."[4]

Sansone and others have offered much evidence that activities as far afield as Sudanese wrestling and Huron lacrosse are "gifts," freely and carefully given in return for some beneficence from nature. As ritualized behavior, sport may have developed stylized, communicative properties that lingered long after their initial functions were forgotten by the participants. Sansone makes interesting connections between a number of "modern" sporting practices and primitive hunting rituals. Some of these include strict dietary regimens, sexual taboos, ablutions with water or oil, filletting of victors, and removal of everyday clothing.[5]

Could it be that the core of modern sport is a timeless, ritual expenditure of energy? How else to explain the fetish that coaches, fans, and players have for "hustling" even if the hustling has little relation to winning? If our modern sports contain practices born of ancient ritual, this may be a key to understanding the widespread attraction of such impractical activities as baseball, football, and basketball. Sansone's argument is intriguing.

At the same time, however, he never fully comes to grips with Mandell or Guttmann, who argue that ritual alone cannot explain the nature of modern sports. For instance, Sansone is silent on sport for women, who have for long epochs lived under cultural systems that denied them such ritual expenditures of energy. Further, one wonders if the essence of sport is so one-dimensional and so fixed through time?[6] There must be a way to reconcile historical continuity with historical change, for if Sansone neglects the importance of "new" features such as records, bureaucracy, and specialization, the modernists may overstate their centrality.

Neither side explains long-term contradictions in sport. These include the mass adulation for star performers, often coupled with bitter disillusionment when stars become egotistical "ingrates"; the passion for victory that seems so inconsistent with indignation over cheating; and the enthusiasm for aggressive play that alternates with outcries against violence. These contradictions are fundamental to the drama of sport. As ancient as they are modern, they have recurred in history, only to be "discovered" by each new generation of commentators.

The notion of the Sportgeist in historical structure offers a model that may reconcile change and continuity in sport history. Without explaining the origins of sport, the model may reveal something about the odd and vexing relationships that connect sports to their historical surroundings. In simple terms this model suggests that any sport exists in at least three interrelated contexts: the Sportgeist, the sport structure, and general structure. Each context has its own pace of historical change, a fact that can create great stresses.

THE SPORTGEIST

The most enduring context, the Sportgeist—or the spirit of sport—exists in any game form. Beneath the different frameworks of rules, conventions, bureaucracies, records, and other assorted forms that have filled the historical record, every sport shares a common core—the Sportgeist. It is simply a set of four polar tensions or contradictions. These exist along dimensions of physicality, competition, creativity, and achievement (figure 1). As individuals or cultures practice game forms, they make choices along these dimensions and thereby animate a particular version of the Sportgeist. Unlike Hegel's notion of the Geist, the Sportgeist does not "realize itself" in history. It is animated or brought to life by human practice. While the Sportgeist contains Hegel's central dimension of freedom, it contains several others. Furthermore, there is no teleology in the Sportgeist. It is only a set of

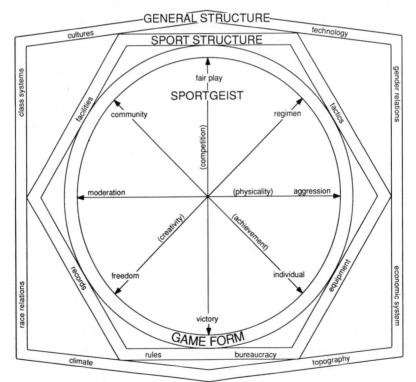

FIGURE 1 SPORTGEIST AND STRUCTURE

potentials, some of which may recur through time. More important, however, is the *existence* of these choices, for this makes the Sportgeist a force of continuity.[7]

The longevity of the Sportgeist, if not its construction, can be shown by reference to ancient sources. A rapid gloss of varied sources is always dangerous, but in this case the sources are used only to reveal the existence of choices along the dimensions of competition, physicality, creativity, and achievement. As early as Homer, one can glimpse some of the internal stresses that form this core spirit of sport.

Victory ⟷ Fair play

The first tension involves the goal of competition. This near timeless tension lies at the heart of any sport. One often finds the quest for victory tugging against fairness or sportsmanship. Both sides existed in ancient Greek athletics. Homer's heroes placed enormous importance on victory, in any contest. The hunger to win is evident among the competitors at the funeral games for Patroklos. At the same time, however, the Sportgeist contains a potential check against easy acceptance of a win-at-all-costs mentality. As Matthew Dickie has cogently demonstrated, competition was tugged back by a sense of fairness and reciprocity. The chariot race is a good example. When young Antilochos captures second place by recklessly endangering himself and Menelaos, he is forced to concede both his unfair tactics and his position. In return, Menelaos shows magnanimity, allowing the youth to keep second prize. Learning from this, Antilochos later most graciously accepts his "loss" to Odysseus in the foot race and thus receives a special prize from Achilles. As Dickie concludes, Homer clearly sets up a balance between winning and what we now call sportsmanship.[8] From the early days of sport, victory has not existed as a goal apart, even if it has received the most attention.

Aggression and Excess ⟷ Moderation and Self-control

Sports are physical contests in which one often finds a clash between efforts to let loose and measures to control the release of physical energy. The choices again appear in Homeric athletic contests. The games for Patroklos include a boxing match that involves Epeios, the personification of unrestrained aggression. Epeios challenges any opponent with the threat: "I will burst his skin and break his bones. And let his supporters remain here in groups to carry him forth when he has suffered defeat at my hands." In the match he bulls Euryalos and scores a KO with a punch that lifts Euryalos off his feet.[9] Aggression did, however, have its limits. Achilles calls off the wrestling match between Odysseus and Ajax, arguing, "Wrestle no more now! Don't wear yourselves out and get hurt." Later the larger congregation of Achaeans intervene with their shouts to stop the combat in arms when Diomedes and Ajax become dangerously aggressive.[10] Throughout history one finds similar tugging between physical aggression and control of it. A steady balance has been difficult to achieve.

Freedom ⟵——————⟶ Regimen

As many observers have noted, sport contains a component of creativity—the "play element" so celebrated by Johan Huizinga. As Huizinga sensed, however, freedom in sport is always jeopardized by routines, techniques, and regimens. This tension is also as old as sport itself.[11] Homer's athletes, like Antilochos, clearly took advantage of opportunities to be creative in the context of competition; but, as happens to any athlete, their ability to be creative had boundaries. Antilochos was guilty of violating a code of fairness—also related to rules—but ancient athletes were also gradually subjected to systems of training and technique that demonstrated the progressively scientific nature of sport, even in the ancient world. One can see the notion of regimen clearly in the areas of rules and training routines.

In the third century A.D. Philostratus collected a mass of training material in his work *On Athletics*. Although the work is historically flawed, it provides evidence of regimen in athletics. Indeed Philostratus believed that his subject was a science as much as music, geometry, military strategy, and medicine. At the same time, Philostratus rejected the excessive rigidity in the "tetrad" system, a four-day training cycle alternating the following: warmup, all out, relax, medium-hard workout. In his words: "How will those who have embraced the tetrad system use it when they come to Olympia where there is dust, just as I have described it, and traditional exercises? Hellanodikai do not train according to a fixed schedule but devise everything on the spot, according to the situation, and the whip awaits a gymnastes who does not follow their instructions."[12] For many centuries, the Sportgeist has contained this difficult choice: freedom to engage in the contest with few restrictions, or constraints in patterns of play regulated by rule, custom, or "science." One has pulled against the other, with little static balance.

Individual ←————————→ Community

Physicality, competition, and creativity are components that flesh out the process of sport as activity. One final dimension has given these activities wider historical significance. This is the ability of sport to represent, at once, the interests of the individual and those of a wider collective. Today we regularly fret about the selfishness of athletes who jump from team to team or of owners who move teams from city to city. Yet each team or city scorned is matched by a team or city elated. Sport has always been a commodity of glory and achievement. Victory is simple to assess in value. For millenia, people have been willing to pay for this glory. The competitors who sacrifice energy and time in the pursuit of glory, to be sure, enjoy as individuals the fruits of victory. At the same time, however, a share of glory in sport has often been pulled back toward the community which the athlete *represents*. Few elements of life and culture contain this ethos of representation, even when the achievement itself is clearly individual.

This duality of achievement is evident in the works of Pindar, whose fifth-century B.C. songs of victory were clearly meant to enhance, on one level, the glory of the individual who commissioned them. Yet at the same time, Pindar made the athlete share glory with both family and polis. As he sang in his eighth Olympian ode to a boy wrestler, "dead men also have a part." Familial glory is a constant theme in Pindar, but so is the glory of the community. Indeed Pindar's songs are sometimes sung to a city-state, as in his second Pythian, written for Hieron but addressed to Hieron's home, Syracuse. It is no coincidence that Hieron was a tyrant, a ruler who lacked traditional legitimacy. Pindar could masterfully assist Hieron by reminding Syracusans of the tyrant's many gifts, including athletic victories.[13]

Later in the same century Alcibiades successfully argued for leadership of an ill-fated campaign by reminding Athenians that his

Olympic chariot victory made "other Hellenes form an idea of our power which even exceeded the reality." Alcibiades shared his achievement with the state, in this case with disastrous results. In a different vein, Isocrates recognized clearly the relationship between individual and community that in its ideal form created a wonderful harmony. At the well-contested athletic event, he argued, "no one passes the time unenthusiastically but each receives that which flatters them, the spectators when they see the athletes working hard for them, and the athletes when they consider that everyone has come to watch them."[14]

As these Greek sources indicate, the Sportgeist—a series of tensions that comprise the spirit of sport—has existed for millenia. At the same time, the choices in the Sportgeist have allowed similar forms of sport to be profoundly different. At its basic level all one needs is a loose membrane of a game form that demands some physical skill. As soon as people begin to play this game form they animate the Sportgeist in infinitely varying ways along the outlined dimensions. Culture may influence a "normal" spirit—perhaps emphasizing victory, aggression, regimen, and community glory—but within any culture each individual invigorates his or her own spirit of sport, which may challenge the boundaries of normal behavior. This allows for change in a constant context.

THE LONGUE DURÉE, INDIVIDUALS, AND THE AMERICAN SPORT INDUSTRY

This Sportgeist, this structure of choices that comprise a core spirit, is part of what Fernand Braudel and the Annales school have called the "longue durée." In Braudel's words:

> The "longue durée" is the endless, inexhaustible history of structures and groups of structures. For the historian a structure is not just a thing built, put together; it also means permanence, sometimes for more than centuries (time too is a structure). This great structure travels through vast tracts of time without changing; if it deteriorates during the long journey, it simply restores itself as it goes along and regains its health, and in the final analysis its characteristics alter only very slowly.

Structures are "set patterns" of thinking and acting which are "a long time dying."[15] Sansone's sportive rituals were and are part of the longue durée. All the axial dimensions of the Sportgeist are part of an inner structure that existed in ancient times and continues to the present. Historians may one day outline a peculiar set of American approaches to physicality, competition, creativity, and achievement as part of the longue durée. Of greater endurance, however, is the structure of choices along these dimensions, which I collectively call the Sportgeist.

If the Sportgeist is a force of continuity, then what explains change within a sport? The answer lies in the relationship of the Sportgeist to other structures that surround it—the sport structure and the general structure. The sport structure is the ensemble of specific rules, tactics, organizations, facilities, records, and equipment through which individuals animate the Sportgeist. As Guttmann and Mandell point out, these structures have continually changed in history. Game forms do change. So do the standard arrangements for competition. Ancient festivals of footraces coordinated by an agonothetes (director of the games) give way to cricket matches promoted by a tavern owner. Even though the stucture of the sport enterprise changes, the Sportgeist tends to linger in its state of constant tension. Rules and tactics may seem cemented in a given instance, but coaches and players still exert freedom within a game to press and stretch the boundaries of convention.

Recognizing the difference between the Sportgeist as one structure, and game forms, bureaucracies, or facilities as another, helps to reconcile the argument that Sansone has with Guttmann and Mandell. They operate at different (although related) levels. Sansone deals with part of the Sportgeist. Mandell and Guttmann focus on the sport structure, although they have some concern for regimen. Their frameworks must be combined for a full understanding of sport in any epoch, but not without one more ingredient. As Mandell argues, sport always exists in relation to a broader environment, which I call a general structure. Here one includes climate, topography, economic systems, class, gender, and race relations. Some elements exhibit Braudel's "permanence"; others are more dynamic. One can uncover their linkages with the sport structure. For instance, Guttmann and Mandell outline the relationship between "modern" sport and the rising scientific and calculating outlook that characterized the Industrial Revolution in Britain. The world of Josiah Wedgewood understandably produced the concept of a sports record and the rationalized management of the Marylebone Cricket Club.

It is not simply a matter of sport "mirroring" society. That model often becomes an exercise in reductionism. Rather, one finds an endless, incalculable series of human actions and decisions over time. People act on the basis of their life situation—their place within the longue durée of structures. Race, class, gender, climate, and economy (to name a few considerations) may each constrain or create opportunity, or cultivate attitudes concerning sports. This experience often inspires a vision of the Sportgeist that may or may not be mainstream. In the same way, the existing sport structure—itself the result of past human actions—may nudge people in certain directions. Depending on their personal vision of the game's spirit, they may try to tear down a brick from the structure or add some mortar to the existing bureaucracy, rules, and systems. Ultimately, such masons of play are often quite frustrated. It is difficult to harness and reproduce through structure a single spirit of the game. Players, fans, and coaches constantly make their own decisions on physicality, achievement, competition, and creativity. These conflicts between the "spirit" of a game and the "letter" of structure occur at all levels, from the sandlot to the major leagues.[16]

While every participant has had a measure of agency in making sport history, I will consider four actors who, between 1860 and 1915, had a profound influence on the structure of American sport. These individuals, one may call them entrepreneurs, acted in the context of the general structure around them. Each tried to harness a personal vision of the Sportgeist in rules, bureaucracies, techniques, or equipment, so that other Americans might reproduce it. At one level they were extremely successful, for these individuals were founders of an industry of "providers," an interlocking network of rules committees, trade associations, manufacturers, retailers, and professional experts. These providers began to develop and sell to the public *preformed* packages of play that included rules, equipment, and expert instructions. Their efforts insured the transformation of informal pastimes into organized, commercialized sports.[17]

This is not, however, a "great man" theory of sport history. Even though the industry could pave the way for some games to become dominant, the individuals who cemented a new sport structure were not as successful in using that structure to harness and spread a particular conception of the Sportgeist. It is one thing to fashion a game form.

It is another to control the spirit that people animate within that game form. The tensions within the Sportgeist—conditioned over centuries through the longue durée—are difficult to control. Thus it was that an industry of providers would experience considerable frustration despite its extensive influence.

The key general structural feature of the period in question was the burgeoning economy of capitalist free enterprise, which could swiftly alter urban landscapes, segmenting residents by class, ethnicity, and race. Supported by major advances in technology, transportation, and communications, the system could fuel rapid economic growth and insure both fabulous wealth for a few and expansion of real income for most. Free enterprise, however, also brought periodic panics and depressions and a widening gap between the richest and poorest, between boss and laborer, between native and immigrant. The last group, such an important force in industrial growth, often symbolized the pressures of madcap change and turmoil, all of which created anxieties about social dissolution, racial exhaustion, and degeneracy. This entire mix provided opportune circumstances for entrepreneurs to develop and market products linked to wholesome exercise, recreation, and sport.[18]

HENRY CHADWICK (1824–1908)

Henry Chadwick, a British immigrant, was acknowledged in his time as the "father of baseball." Among the first inductees to the Hall of Fame, Chadwick was never more than an adequate player. His claim to immortality, rather, lay in his work as a journalist. Indeed, it is fair to say that Chadwick invented the role of modern sports journalist, a role integral to the operation of the contemporary industry.

Born in 1824 in Exeter, England, Chadwick moved with his family to the United States when he was thirteen and lived until 1908 in and about Brooklyn. Since his father, James, was editor of the *Western Times,* it is no surprise that Henry had drifted into newspaper work by the time he was twenty. From his earliest days with the *Long Island Star,* his career goal was simple: to make a living promoting sports, especially baseball, as a wholesome form of recreation. He wrote for the *New York Times, Brooklyn Eagle, New York Herald,* New York *Clipper, Sporting Life,* and *Sporting News,* to name his most prominent outlets. From 1860 to 1881 he edited the *Beadle (Dime) Base-Ball Player*, and when that dissolved he continued as editor of the *Spalding Official Baseball Guide* until his death. He was a recognized authority on rules, a status strengthened by his membership on the rules committees of the earliest national baseball association. He invented much of the system now used to score games and statistics. In short, he was a prolific writer and promoter.[19]

Chadwick is typically described as commanding and dignified in presence, his paternal demeanor symbolized in his long white beard. His personal manner evidently matched his formal, high-toned, but enthusiastic prose. Chadwick was a moralist and baseball was his theater. In an early instructional book, he recalled discovering his life's work while watching a cricket match in 1856. He decided that baseball could do for the United States what cricket had done for England, namely be "a powerful lever . . . by which our people could be lifted into a position of more devotion to physical exercise and healthful outdoor recreation than they had hitherto, as a people, been noted for."[20]

Chadwick's concerns were largely a function of his existence in an urban environment undergoing drastic transformations. Reformers of all stripes looked for moral elixirs to reduce the apparent chaos and disorder of urban life. Chadwick joined many in championing wholesome sports. For example, he argued in 1866 that "as a remedy for the many evils resulting from the immoral association boys and young men of our cities are apt to become connected with, the game merits the endorsement of every clergyman in the country." His claims for sports also extended to their health benefits. As he proudly asserted (whether true or not), baseball and sports in general had taught "the mercantile community of our large cities that 'all work and no play' is the most costly policy they can pursue, both in regard to the advantages to their own health, and in the improvement in the work of their employees."[21]

Chadwick's mission of reform through sport led him to concoct his own design for the Sportgeist, which he attempted to harness throughout his lifetime by tinkering with the structure of rules, styles of play, and league administration. Predictably, his attempts yielded only partial and temporary successes.

Perhaps the most important of Chadwick's crusades was his continued effort to promote technical regimen, the "science" that he and his ilk were creating. He had a personal stake in selling instructional guidebooks, but his argument went further. He maintained that one could enjoy baseball's full benefits of morality, health, and manliness only by playing at sophisticated levels, which required close attention to rules, tactics, strategy, and training. He constantly praised the growing sciences of hitting, fielding, and pitching. They alone distinguished the real sport from just another kids' game. [22]

Such a position toward the Sportgeist naturally led him to approach the sport structure in certain ways. A champion of regimen, technical prowess, and expertise, Chadwick was also an early proponent of professionalism. As Melvin Adelman has argued, if the activities themselves are wholesome, it is difficult to deny pursuing them at a professional level. Indeed, Chadwick wrote late in life that professionalism "proved to be of great use in perfecting the game, and in developing its scientific features." He continually pressed for rule changes—such as the "fly rule"—that would make the game a test of mental and moral as well as physical courage. [23]

The Sportgeist, however, contains elements of freedom and physicality that frustrated Chadwick's scientific vision. For instance, he regretted the rise of the slugging game, later so personified by Babe Ruth. In 1905 he saw trouble in the increasing neglect of the fine points of batting. "Too much attention," he wrote, "is given to the method of batting known as 'slugging for homers,' a habit that marks what is called 'record batting,' which takes the place of what is called 'teamwork at the bat.'" Chadwick never had time to cement such cracks in baseball's scientific regimen. [24]

He also constantly pressed another aspect of the Sportgeist— sportsmanship. As David Voigt has argued, Chadwick joined another British "father" of the game, Harry Wright, in championing the cause that "British standards of sportsmanship should dominate organized baseball." Sportsmanship was part of the broader morality play that Chadwick had earlier transferred from cricket to baseball. In his mind cricket taught "a love of order, discipline, and fair play," all of which made it far more than mere exercise or play. Baseball was no different. [25]

The realities of competition, however, often tugged in a different direction. Chadwick's vision was constantly sullied in his eyes by players, coaches, fans, and media who "kicked" or protested against the calls of the umpire. As he wrote in a letter to the editor of *Sporting Life* in 1887, hissing by fans made no sense. "What good does it do? Not a particle in any respect. On the contrary, it acts against good umpiring, and is encouraging to that nuisance of our ball fields—kicking." Chadwick would not countenance kicking as a tactic for winning. Obviously, many Americans did. They accepted most of his structure; much less of his spirit. Some fellow journalists were no different. They were undaunted by Chadwick's furious criticism of "cowardly" writers guilty of abusing umpires in print.[26]

This was a long crusade for an ardent crusader. Near the end of his life, in an interview with *Harper's Weekly*, he included "kicking" as the most recent "abuse" that threatened the integrity of the professional game. Such "rowdy blackguardism" had grown, he claimed, because of the "laxity in discipline on the part of club-team managers and the aid and countenance given the managers and their players by the majority of the magnates." Chadwick ended with mixed feelings about the prospects of sportsmanship. While Ban Johnson had brought a new moral tenor to league administration, too many "poorly managed" teams failed to make their punishments fit the crime. The problem continues today: the late Billy Martin took "kicking" literally, with little punishment.[27]

Chadwick fought other structural battles in his day—for rule changes to improve the "scientific" balance between offense and defense, alterations in the scoring system, and policies to eliminate the strong gambling element that threatened to leave the professional game stillborn. Despite his failure to harness his ideal Sportgeist, he earned a rightful place as the father of the game. More importantly, he helped to shape the foundations of an industry by creating the role of insider journalist. Like so many writers and reporters who followed him in the rise of sport, he was part of the action—on the field and off—that he described to the public. He not only wrote the news, he made it. Equally important, his columns and books conveyed to readers that the real world of sports did not come from the fantasies of sandlot players who made up rules as they went along. Rather, the public should consume preformed games that were developed, packaged, and delivered by an industry of providers.

Chadwick was a fountain of rules, techniques, records, and lore. He and his colleagues would be the mediums of knowledge between those inside the sport structure and the marketplace outside. As he wrote in his 1868 instructional book, the successful consumer would be the careful reader. Any studious reader could gain a "pretty good idea of the game" by perusing his book. On the other hand, he warned, "if he be one of those careless readers who merely glance at a book and swallow its contents, as they do their meals, bolting without tasting, he need not expect much benefit from it." In the hands of experts like Chadwick, the structure of sport was changing and becoming more complex.[28]

ALBERT GOODWILL SPALDING (1850–1915)

In 1899 Chadwick wrote in the first issue of the *Sporting Goods Dealer* that "our Yankee manufacturers now control the supply of sport goods the world over." The growth of the sporting goods industry had been immense during the same years that Chadwick had written his numerous columns. The rise of sports journalism clearly was linked to the growth of the sporting goods industry; their relationship was symbiotic. Journalists like Chadwick conveyed expertise and regimen in print. Sporting goods manufacturers and dealers mirrored this with material objects. One would hardly have thrived without the other.[29]

The central goal of this relationship was standardization. For this purpose Chadwick had a strong ally and associate, the fellow Hall of Famer and sporting goods magnate Albert Goodwill Spalding. As Spalding's biographer, Peter Levine, has argued splendidly, Spalding was very much part of a middle class trying to find ways to reorder a world seething with rapid growth and change, strange new faces and languages, violent confrontations over work and life conditions, and underlying fears that an old American breed had lost its vigor. Echoing many American historians, Levine writes that one remedy lay in "rational procedures devised by experts to bring order and control to every area of American life." Spalding took Chadwick's regimen two steps further: into the bureaucratic control of teams and players and into the rationalized production of equipment.[30]

Born in 1850 in the rural village of Byron, Illinois, Spalding came of age in Rockford, a rail station about one hundred miles west of Chicago. Bitten by the infectious baseball bug of the day, he quickly developed a reputation as a crack pitcher, and in 1865 he was invited to join the "Forest City's," a team newly formed by local business boosters who hoped to promote their town through baseball. The Forest City's competed within the loosely organized National Association of Baseball Players, giving Spalding exposure to the big leagues. He caught the eye of Harry Wright, manager of the famous Cincinnati Red Stockings, and Wright convinced the young pitcher to join him in jumping in 1871 to the Boston team of the new National Association of Professional Baseball Players. Spalding pitched brilliantly for five seasons in Boston, helping the Red Stockings to four consecutive championships, 1872–75. In July of 1875, however, this industrious, sober professional—the type that Chadwick worked so hard to promote—committed his second sin of "revolving," or team jumping. He signed a contract to be player-manager for 1876 with the Chicago White Stockings. Lured to Chicago by coal merchant William Hulbert, Spalding not only shored up the franchise with other defectors, but also helped Hulbert create the National League of Professional Baseball Clubs.[31]

Spalding pressed a design of regimen on all players and teams that wanted to be a part of professional baseball. The National League was arguably America's first serious sports bureaucracy, with hard rules on player contracts, franchise locations, game management, and scheduling. For an old "revolver," Spalding became a hard-line critic of "overpaid players" who were only interested in "their own aggrandisement."[32] He successfully led wars against several rival leagues, including one organized by the players' union. His work with the National League was essential to the creation of a model sports bureaucracy. Yet Spalding's venture into sporting goods had a much more profound effect on the development of an industry of providers, thanks to his promotion of expertise, standardization, and bureaucracy.

Spalding opened his sporting goods business in March of 1876, with his brother, J. Walter, as partner. It was a small retail operation but it grew quickly through sound financial and marketing strategies. These included backward integration into manufacturing, a decisive move in a time when most name-brand sporting goods were the products of contracts between retailers and silent manufacturers. The Spalding brothers, however, knew the economies that existed in integrated manufacture and distribution. Within two decades the firm of A. G. Spalding and Bros. dominated a strong field of rivals that included Rawlings, Reach, Wright and Ditson, Meacham Arms, McClean, and many others. Indeed Spalding had silently acquired several rivals, who continued to sell goods under their own brand names. The Spalding name itself, however, circulated widely, in many sports, with equipment produced in specialty factories around the country, and sold through Spalding or allied retail outlets or through the mail.[33]

The Spaldings certainly sought market share for their own brand name, but in so doing they also promoted the larger industry of providers and experts. Advertisements sent a clear message that homemade games and handcrafted equipment would no longer do in an industrial age. For instance, in the spring of 1893, the firm ran a series of clever ads in the *Sporting News*. Each week the commentary supplemented cartoons illustrating the hazards of inferior equipment and the value of genuine Spalding balls, chest protectors, bats, and shoes. One notice describing Spalding bats began with a story about a pathetic "crank" who could not even hit a ball until his team captain insisted that he throw away the "Jonah" bat that was fashioned by a "wheelwright up in the country." Likewise there was the hapless runner who staggered between bases in clodhoppers habitually bought "from some inexperienced cobbler." As the advertisement warned, a cobbler might be able to help with some things, but "not with Base Ball shoes." This was the fundamental message of all manufacturers, and it echoed all of Chadwick's lines. Sports were a specialized product not to be entrusted to the hands of oldstyle craftsmen, whether they worked in leather, wood, or words.[34]

The Spaldings did not wait for others to join this chorus. They aggressively led the field. One of their shrewdest practices was the publication of guidebooks edited by prominent experts like Henry Chadwick. The earliest guidebooks in baseball had been issued by general publishing houses like Beadle and DeWitt. This changed in 1876 when the Spaldings began to publish their own guide, filled with the National League rules, records, history, instruction, and lots of advertisements for Spalding products. By 1885 they were ready to launch their Library of American Sports, intended to educate the public in a variety of sports. This venture was so successful that the Spaldings created a subsidiary firm in 1892, the American Sports Publishing Company. With James E. Sullivan as president, this publishing house produced hundreds of guidebooks and publications on an impressive range of sports.[35]

Making and selling guidebooks became standard practice in the sporting goods industry. Smart retailers advertised the availability of guidebooks in their "depots." R. E. Dimick, a St. Louis dealer, noted in a February, 1889 issue of the *Sporting News* that "we make a specialty of sporting books of every description. They are very good to have when settling disputes." Sporting goods firms were selling inexpensive, standardized packages of expert knowledge that linked sporting goods to game forms. One could buy booklets by experts who would convey the intricacies of tennis, football, skating, croquet, and baseball in their finest detail.[36]

Involving scattered experts and scientists of sport could give products legitimacy. It would not, however, ensure the levels of authority that the Spaldings sought in the marketplace. For this they needed closer alignment with young governing bodies like the National League or the Intercollegiate Football Association. They found this through tie-ins as the manufacturer of "official" equipment. Their efforts began, as always, in baseball, where in the late 1870s they wrestled the official ball away from the L. H. Mahn Company of Boston. This began a long, aggressive campaign of negotiating the rights to produce both the official rules and guidebooks and the official equipment in a vast range of sports at all levels, from the playground league to the National League. Such tie-ins benefited both sides.

A good example is the Intercollegiate Football Association whose guiding spirit was Walter Camp. The early rules, from 1876 to the mid-1880s, were privately printed in Princeton. By 1887, however, they were published by Wright and Ditson, a sporting goods firm willing to try new markets such as tennis and football. In 1891 an interesting turn occurred. The Spaldings took over the publication of the rules in this, the first year of their silent partnership with Wright and Ditson. Wright and Ditson could continue to sell their name-brand goods, but they could not continue to publish an increasingly valuable guidebook.[37]

A year later, the Spaldings captured the most valuable tie-in of all—official status for their name-brand football. Prior to this, the official ball had been a British import, hardly acceptable for a chauvinist like A. G. Spalding. In May, 1892, however, the association voted to make the Spalding No. J Foot-ball an official ball with the further stipulation that "all matches of the Association must be played" with such a ball. The company wisely cemented its relationship to the IFA by retaining Walter Camp as editor of the annual guidebook and by selling

Spalding equipment to Yale at a discount. All of this was helped by Julian Curtiss, a Spalding executive, who happened to be a Yale alumnus and friend of Camp's. When necessary, Curtiss had no qualms about asking Camp's predictions on rule changes that might affect Spalding equipment such as the "head harness."[38]

Camp, the IFA, and the Spalding firm all enjoyed increased authority through this kind of relationship, represented in mutual endorsements. Just as an endorsement helped the tangible goods in the marketplace, so too did "official" goods provide legitimacy and authority for the distant endorsers. Walter Camp grasped this principle firmly. Describing football in his *Book of College Sports*, he cautioned that "it is best that players should never use anything but the regulation ball," either the British "J. Lillywhite" or the American "Spalding." He also insisted, however, that the regulation ball "should bear the stamp, '*Adopted by the Intercollegiate Foot-ball Association*'" (my emphasis).[39] The sale of every Spalding ball paid interest to Camp's young association, for every person who bought an official IFA ball likely bought into Camp's basic version of the game.

A. G. Spalding suffered few setbacks in his business career. His dogged pursuit of standardized games, products, and leagues clearly lent force to a Sportgeist weighted toward regimen. At the same time, his practices in the sporting goods market set off other forces that frustrated his visions of a disciplined labor force. Part of his conception of the Sportgeist rested on an orderly community, managed by capitalists for private profit and public amusement. He became a champion of loyalty to contract and community. There was an underlying problem, however, in the ties between experts and sporting goods. Experts garner their own status and prestige, just as they produce market share for the products they endorse. Spalding aggressively sought star players as individual product endorsers. It was a distinct irony that his use of star endorsements nurtured individualism, which continued to haunt professional sports in the forms of contract jumping and contract holdouts. Further, players who recognized their value in the market for goods created their own collectives to fight the magnates for higher wages. Spalding's empire in sporting goods fuelled a part of the Sportgeist that ran headlong against his own peculiar vision of the compliant athlete.

JAMES E. SULLIVAN (1860–1914)

One of the most important cogs in the Spalding machine was James E. Sullivan. Although best known today as a founder of the Amateur Athletic Union (AAU) and the person for whom an annual award to the nation's outstanding amateur athlete is named, Sullivan is a much more interesting character than this. As indicated in his *Dictionary of American Biography* profile, "in reality he was the first sports czar." This is no exaggeration. Whatever the extent of his power, it rested on his near unique position at the intersection of journalism, sporting goods, and the emerging sports bureaucracies.[40]

Sullivan was born in New York City in 1860, the son of Irish immigrants. His father, a construction foreman for the New York Central Railroad, could not offer him more than a public school education. This was enough to launch James Sullivan on a career in journalism, which he began in 1878 with the house of Frank Leslie. He also flirted with sports journalism, starting a short-lived *Athletic News* in 1880, heading the sports department of the *Morning Journal*, and working with John P. Day on the *Sporting Times*. His major break came when he was hired by the Spaldings in 1892 to run their newly organized subsidiary, the American Sports Publishing Company (ASPC).[41]

The Spaldings certainly recognized his multiple qualities, for by this time he was an established figure in amateur athletic circles. A prominent member of the Pastime Athletic Club since 1877, he had thrown his hat in with the founders of the Amateur Athletic Union (1888), whose objective was to wrest control of amateur sport from the established National Association of Amateur Athletes of America. From 1889 until his death in 1914, Sullivan served as an officer in the AAU. More importantly, he was to the AAU what Spalding was to the National League—the pit bull who could fight tenaciously in an age of recurring struggle between competing organizations. As John Lucas has concluded, Sullivan was "a blunt, no-nonsense pragmatist who avoided compromise and subterfuge, preferring an honest directness— no matter who it hurt."[42]

Although lacking some of the style one would expect from a successful bureaucrat, Sullivan evidently learned the art of compromise, for his bureaucratic portfolio was massive. In the decade before his death he served as a senior official of the AAU and president of one of its regional groups, the Metropolitan Association; chairman of the New York Public Recreation Commission; a member of the New York Board of Education; three-time American commissioner to the Olympic Games; and as director of the athletic events associated with the Buffalo Pan-American Exposition of 1901, the St. Louis Exposition (and Olympics) of 1904, and the Jamestown Exposition of 1907. For a short time in 1911, he was chairman of the newly formed New York Athletic Commission. This only begins to describe his activities at the center of the movement to organize American sport and recreation. All of this activity complemented his work for the Spaldings.

He was a man on a mission to organize the vast frontiers of sports lying beyond the pale of professionals and collegians. His objectives were colored by his own experience and by his perceptions of the world around him. His world vision seemed shaped by factors of racism, nationalism, and a quest for bourgeois respectability, not an unusual combination in his day. For instance, he wrote in an extended ASPC *Athletic Primer* (1907) that the athletic boom had occurred because "the doctors, teachers, and college presidents, all interested in the future of our race, have come to the conclusion that outdoor life is sure to benefit mankind."[43]

For Sullivan, the notion of race blended with his sense of nationalism. As John Lucas noted, "he would remain an aggressive American patriot until his death." He continually trumpeted the performances of American athletes in international competition. Writing in 1901 for *Cosmopolitan,* he proudly recalled Albert Spalding's boast of bringing to the Paris Games of 1900 "the finest specimens of mankind that could be provided throughout the civilized world." The next year's Pan-American games at Buffalo, claimed Sullivan, merely showed again "the supremacy of the American Athlete." International competition was something Americans should pursue with the same aggressive spirit they used in warfare. Indeed, he made the analogy explicit in 1907, when he tried to pressure the Congress for a one hundred thousand-dollar appropriation to the Olympic team. As he stated in the *Times,* "the Nation should provide the sinews of war where the issue at stake is National and not individual." This was one battle he lost, even with Theodore Roosevelt as honorary president of the Olympic committee.[44]

Although Sullivan lacked the president's social status, this did not prevent him from living out the quest for respectability so prominent among budding bureaucrats of his day. The amateur athletic movement was a status vehicle, for common interests allowed elites to rub elbows in limited ways with men like Sullivan. His *Primer* stressed the importance of "gentlemen, leading citizens and business men" to the organization and success of the amateur movement. His model club would allow no gambling or liquor sales and would operate a blackball system in member selection. He shared the views of his friend, William B. Curtis, who wrote in the AAU's early days that amateur rules alone would not protect a respectable contest. "Many corner-loafers and bullies from the slums have never transgressed the amateur definition," Curtis argued, and "thieves, garroters, burglars, incendiaries, forgers, murderers—and even cigarette smokers—are frequently qualified amateurs under the strictest rules ever framed." [45]

Sullivan's mission, however, was not elitist. In his quest to organize, he had a vision of a massive triangle, with a huge base at the playground, YMCA, and schoolyard levels, tapering off at the top with the international competitors. He argued that the AAU should be broad-based and that "athletics should be for the masses and not for the classes," provided that the masses were organized under the AAU structure of bourgeois respectability. [46]

Sullivan's image of the Sportgeist was a combination of emphases on regimen (especially as found in AAU policies and Spalding guides), victory, and community, these last two fused in his quest for American supremacy in international competition. As did his counterparts in this study, he tried to harness his spirit of sport by altering and expanding structures. As president of the American Sports Publishing Company he continually promoted regimen by extending the influence of experts whom he hired to write various guides and primers. Chadwick was one of his prime authors. So was Walter Camp. When the marketplace of football expertise was threatened in 1894 by a rival publication involving Amos Alonzo Stagg, Sullivan urged Camp to write a quick fifty-page book on "How to Play Football" so as to "kill the sales" of the Stagg book. Expert coaches like Camp were at the heart of Sullivan's athletic revolution. In summing up America's staggering success at the Stockholm Olympics of 1912, Sullivan reminded his readers that "it is coaching—more than anything else—that puts us in a class far above the other countries." [47]

Moreover, expertise had to be fully developed in bureaucratic structure. Hence Sullivan devoted most of his energy to cementing the authority of the AAU in the athletic marketplace. He had a hand in designing the notion of an athletic "sanction," which gave the union some monopoly powers. An athlete participating in an unsanctioned, non-college event, sponsored by a non-AAU organization, ran the risk of losing eligibility for all AAU events. As the union's control widened, the sanction had greater weight. Sullivan tightened the screws even further in 1896 with his scheme to force all athletes to register and pay a fee to the AAU. As Robert Korsgaard put it, "It became almost a fetish for the A.A.U. to control and inhibit the movement of athletes." Sullivan and his colleagues "wanted to know who [the] athletes were, what their capabilities were, who they represented, where they resided, which meets they entered, and how effectively to control all the contingencies that would arise out of the answers to these problems." [48]

Sullivan recognized the limits to the union's jurisdiction, however, and he never took on the forces of college athletics directly, although he skirmished on the basketball front. More important to him was the need for a powerful bureaucracy within the colleges that could work with the AAU. To this end he wrote several times to Camp urging him to form an "association for the government of all sports that the colleges take up, make your own rules and have articles of affiliation with the A.A.U." Later, he saw no immediate threat from the young Intercollegiate Athletic Association, soon to be the National Collegiate Athletic Association (NCAA). They were "clever people" who saw that there was only one broad-based governing body, "and that's the A.A.U." [49]

Sullivan never lived to see the bitter battles between his organization and the NCAA. For him, the experts had to stick together. At the height of a 1909 football controversy, when violent play threatened the gridiron's existence in many schools and colleges, Sullivan came to the defense of the rules committee. Men like Camp, Stagg, and Parke Davis, he told the *New York Times*, were "men of common sense." Moreover, they were the experts. The worst road to reform, he cautioned, was to have "honest intentioned people who are slightly ignorant of what football actually is" constantly "hammer away" at the rules committee, "without having any very definite idea as to what should be done." [50]

Sullivan respected his social superiors only if they deferred to his expertise in sport. The industry could be open to the masses and favored by gentlemen and college presidents, but it should be controlled by middle class expert bureaucrats like James E. Sullivan. Such an attitude blended well with Sullivan's quest for national victory. His feud with the British establishment after the 1908 London games and his estrangement from Baron De Coubertin reflect his antagonism to anyone obstructing his vision, even if the obstructionists were his social superiors. He railed against England's Amateur Athletic Association (AAA) for its alleged prejudice against the American runners Hayes and Carpenter. Naming specific individuals, he found their conduct "cruel, unsportsmanlike, and absolutely unfair." More significant, he charged that the AAA was "working under the old customs," and not in tune with the latest methods of expert administration. Incompetence was more of an indictment than lack of sportsmanship.[51]

In his long battle with Coubertin, Sullivan never showed deference to the baron's nobility or to his paternal position in the international spectacle of athleticism, the Olympics. Coubertin might have founded the games, but in Sullivan's estimation he could not run them. He directly accused the baron of being an "inept leader," and constantly challenged the authority of the International Olympic Committee. How could the "lovely gentleman," Professor William Milligan Sloane, be a member, Sullivan complained to the baron, when "he knows absolutely nothing about athletics."[52]

Sullivan's irritation was soothed by the continued dominance of the American teams. After America's near sweep at Stockholm, the *Nation* was moved to suggest that the English were having second thoughts about their casual approach to competition. With the English press calling the poor showing at Stockholm a "national disgrace," the *Nation* argued that England faced the alternatives of either adopting America's approach to expert and professional coaching and administration, or of "resigning any hope of regaining his old prestige in the world of sport."[53]

This bubble of superiority soon burst. Within months, news surfaced that Jim Thorpe, decathlon victor at Stockholm, had once played baseball for pay. Sullivan expressed shock and outrage. Thorpe was stripped of all his records (and quickly of his medals), but he was less to blame than those who had for so long stayed silent about his transgressions. Indignantly, Sullivan and two colleagues publicly wrote that they had extended widespread publicity about the Olympic team selections. It seemed "strange that men having knowledge of Mr. Thorpe's professional conduct did not at such time, *for the honor of their country* [my emphasis], come forward and place in the hands of the American committee such information as they had."[54] There should have been no shock. Men like Sullivan had fostered a spirit that emphasized victory as foremost. National pride came in winning, not in eliminating the world's greatest athlete. If Thorpe was exposed after the victory, what did it matter? A win was still a win.

Sullivan succeeded in nudging Americans to accept greater bureaucracy and regimen in the pursuit of victory and national pride. As the Thorpe saga illustrated, however, this came at a price. For Sullivan, there were also some personal costs. He was never welcomed into the "old boys' fraternity," the International Olympic Committee. Respectability went only so far.[55]

SENDA BERENSON (1868–1954)

Sullivan never lost his faith in the experts whom he saw as guardians of all that was right in sport, and he extended this belief into the realm of women's athletics. Indeed, he went so far as to argue in 1910 that men had no place running women's sports. Unlike earlier times, he claimed, today "we have thousands of capable young women teachers . . . well qualified to coach and manage girls' teams, and whose judgement of girls' teams is much better than that of the average man." He had in mind women like Senda Berenson.[56]

In an outstanding monograph on American women's sport history, Cindy Himes examines the attempts by female physical educators to establish a separate sphere in athletics. Their efforts began to coalesce in the 1890s at the "Seven Sister" institutions, which included Vassar, Smith, Wellesley, and Bryn Mawr. Unlike wealthy participants at elite country clubs and resorts, the directors of physical education at these institutions did not have the social prestige that allowed for eccentricities like active sports. College women came under considerable attack for engaging in games that were commonly seen as a male preserve. "As a result," says Himes, "female physical educators modified athletics for women in an attempt to dissociate them from rites of masculinity. The result was the college athletic festival which linked sports with a celebration of traditional feminine qualities."[57]

These middle-class educators were sensitive to the conservative diatribes that readily associated the athletic woman with social, political, and sexual aberrations. This was a particular threat to women like Senda Berenson at Smith, Constance Applebee at Bryn Mawr, and Lucille Eaton Hill at Wellesley. Therefore, as Himes demonstrates, these pioneer physical educators modified athletics to defend their own as well as their students' identities.

It was logical then that these women pressed a particular version of the Sportgeist stressing sportsmanship, moderation, and community over victory, excess, and individualism. One finds this clearly stated in Lucille Eaton Hill's introduction to *Athletics and Outdoor Sports for Women*, a book in hot demand at the Boston Athenaeum in 1903. As Hill stressed, "Our ever present ideal should be Health and Beauty; and during this early stage of our experience in athletics our watchword should be 'Moderation.'"[58]

A classic attempt at fashioning a Sportgeist through adaptations of rules may be found in the sport of basketball. Himes notes that such modifications were a "common way" of dissociating women's sports from the masculine realm; but, as Himes also argues, "rule modifications did not spring from a social vacuum."[59] Rather they incorporated the reactions by Senda Berenson (who first adapted basketball for women) and her colleagues to contemporary sentiment about female capacities.

Senda Berenson was born in 1868 in Lithuania. A Jewish immigrant, whose father earned a living peddling pots and pans in Boston, she was hardly an elite sportswoman. Yet she well represents the cohort of early physical educators who erected an alternative model of athletics in schools and colleges. She received her formal training at the Boston Normal School of Gymnastics under the direction of Amy Morris Homans. In January, 1892 she began two decades of service at Smith College.[60]

One ex-student recalled Berenson as "that little figure calling directions in that soft yet staccato foreign voice [who] fascinated and compelled us." Photos in the Smith College archives support this image. They reveal a woman of moderate, almost slight figure, dark, wavy hair pulled back in a bun, dark eyes and a gentle visage. Berenson does not appear as a dominating or commanding presence. Rather she seems a confident and sympathetic figure who gained respect through intelligence and good will.[61]

Berenson saw the value of sport as part of a larger physical culture movement that might ameliorate historical conditions afflicting women. She shared with Walter Camp and others a fear that modern industrial life was somehow softening the species, especially in America. Her lecture notes contain warnings such as: "Our women are becoming thin—anaemic—neurotic—nerveless, sexless creatures—a menace to our future civilization." American women needed a "new birth" that would rekindle "primitive instincts" such as could be found in the "delight and abandon in games, the joy of the genuine simple things in life." Women needed stronger constitutions for more than simple reproductive capacities. They needed strength and courage "now that the woman's sphere of usefulness is constantly widening, now that she is proving that her work in certain fields of labor is equal to man's work and hence should have equal reward, now that all fields of labor and all professions are opening their doors to her. . . ."[62]

Like many physical educators of her generation, Berenson discovered that sports were an important adjunct to gymnastic exercise. As she wrote to one college benefactor, "carefully supervised games" could develop, "as no formal gymnastics may," characteristics such as self-reliance, self-control and teamwork, all of which were "so necessary to the modern woman." Her emphasis, however, was always on the term "carefully supervised," a facet of women's athletics that she and her colleagues believed set their games apart from the men's.[63] Her goal was nothing less than a realignment of the Sportgeist. Her personal focus was the sport of basketball.

In the fall of 1892 Berenson introduced the new sport to her students. She had read the rules of the new game in *Physical Education*, the magazine of the Young Men's Christian Association. James Naismith had invented the game in nearby Springfield around the time of her arrival at Smith. As she later wrote, "In all probability, Dr. Naismith had no idea it would ever be played by women." Indeed, Berenson's girls did not play the same game. Her rule modifications attempted to stretch the Sportgeist away from the poles of physical aggression and individual glory.[64]

Physical moderation was clearly a goal. Her rules prohibited snatching or batting the ball away from an opponent, for instance. Berenson approvingly quoted one observer of her modified rules who wrote that "the important lesson of this game, and the one that should make it a memorable one, is that a courteous consideration of an opponent, even in an antagonistic game, does not necessarily diminish a team's chances for victory." In a similar attempt to insure moderation, she divided the court into three sections, the special domains of "guards," "centers," or "homes." Players in each position could only pass the ball beyond the dividing line.[65]

While the court restrictions were aimed in part at preventing overexertion, they were also intended to prevent domination of the game by a few outstanding individuals. The same intent lay behind the rule prohibiting more than three dribbles. Berenson was aiming to avoid the creation of stars, who represented individualism.

As Himes has shown, Berenson and her colleagues wanted to protect their young charges from criticism about unfeminine behavior. They also knew they must erect an effective organizational structure if they were to have any hope of braking the forces that nudged men's sport toward excess, physicality, individualism, and unbridled competition. They achieved this for a time by playing the game of structure as well as their male counterparts.

By 1899 there were so many versions of modified rules that interested female directors formed the Committee on Women's Basketball Rules to achieve some synthesis. Senda Berenson was appointed editor. Equally important, the committee entered into an arrangement with James Sullivan to have the rules published in a special guidebook, *Basket Ball for Women*. As always, the agreement resulted in a privileged position for Spalding equipment. The rules declared both the Spalding ball and the Spalding goal as official items. Be that as it may, the committee now had instant national circulation as well as the Spalding stamp of authority. Berenson clearly recognized her power as editor of the guidebook. As she recalled in a later speech, she made it a special point to enlist "good people" to write articles in the pamphlet on good sportsmanship.[66]

Whenever possible Berenson promoted her alternative vision of an athletics structure that might prevent the objectionable aspects of competition. Her lecture notes include the main elements of her approach: no interschool games, no fees for admission, audience by invitation only, something social always after games, no chewing gum, tidy appearance (hair in ribbons or braids). One might add to this an additional restriction: the games should be *by women for women*. Few men were allowed to attend. As Himes notes, the performances were almost rituals supporting a female vision of life. There was no need for leering, cynical men on the sidelines. One of Berenson's handwritten notices survives in the Smith College archives. It reads:

> NOTICE ! !
> Gentlemen are not
> allowed in the
> gymnasium during
> basket ball games
> S. Berenson

She appears to have been effective on this front. One 1895 newspaper account of the annual contest between the freshman and sophomore first teams, commonly known at Smith as The Game, notes that only a handful of male dignitaries were present, including the college president. "The spectacle," cracked the reporter, "would have stirred the heart of Anthony Comstock," a well-known champion of purity. Berenson's approach to athletics for women represents the core of the alternative model that reached full expression several decades later.[67]

Women's athletics could be something of a public, female "sphere of influence," to use Berenson's own phrase. A separate women's sports establishment might parallel the contemporary growth of other institutions run by women—settlements, trade unions, and, of course, colleges. As Linda Kerber has recently argued, "in each case, the refusal to merge their groups into male-dominated institutions gave women not only crucial practical and political experience, but also a place where they could rest the levers with which they hoped to effect social change." In this case women's sport might be a special arena nurturing public displays of community, fair play, and moderation.[68]

Berenson's model rested on a foundation of intramural competition, which she and others hoped would reduce the excesses rampant in men's intercollegiate rivalries. On close inspection, however, one can find small stress fractures in this framework. For every measure of teamwork, sportsmanship, and self-control, the Sportgeist included equal potential for individualism and unrestrained pursuit of victory. Like Chadwick, Spalding, and Sullivan, Berenson might influence the organization of play, but she could not ensure that her structure yielded uniformity in practice or consistency in spirit. Specifically, the evidence suggests a greater than expected promotion of individual glory and victory.

Almost immediately, the competing classes enlisted scribes who churned out fight songs glorifying their selected heroines. One mid-nineties freshman contingent sang the following to the tune of "Hold the Fort":

> Hold the ball, for Ware is coming.
> Tallant signals still,
> Tillie Blaikie's in the center,
> Win we must and will.

Berenson prohibited the "class yells" that she associated with Bloody Monday–style campus events, but she allowed these "songs." The evidence suggests that students sang these paeans with total abandon. At times, group solidarity seemed a vehicle for enlarging individual status. Moreover, songs and colors helped to stir up class rivalries. Organizers draped the gymnasium with bunting, ribbons, flags, and flowers of the chosen hue. As one local account of the first big game put it, "It is impossible to describe the scrambling and hullabaloo that took place." These games were by all accounts highly contested and well supported.[69]

The annual game quickly became one of the most important events on campus. One 1895 report claims that "seats were in such high demand that $15 was paid for a single one." Apparently Berenson could not prevent scalping, and scalpers would have had a field day working the long line of students who waited for over an hour to find a spot in the small gym. By 1896 the *New York Times* even claimed that faculty had "discussed giving up the annual game on account of the strong class feeling shown."[70] These experiences suggest the difficulty of reproducing a narrow vision of the Sportgeist. Some Smith women seemed to want more than Berenson could give them. While they never toppled the structures of moderate play that surrounded them, one can find evidence that some college women pressed on the boundaries, in search of something closer to the dreaded "male model."

Berenson and her colleagues reacted by building structure. In

1905 the old Women's Basketball Rules Committee became the *National* Women's Basketball Rules Committee, which in 1917 melded with the Committee on Women's Athletics (CWA) within the American Physical Education Association. The CWA was complemented in 1923 by the women's division of the National Amateur Athletic Federation. In subsequent decades both groups pressed on women's athletics a platform stressing sportsmanship and enjoyment over individual accomplishment or winning. These scions of Berenson's committee vigorously asserted the need for women to control their own model of athletics, one that stressed competition in "play days" rather than in direct interschool contests.

Their control of athletics, however, was never complete. Many women played under men's rules. Between the world wars, women athletes competed under male control in the AAU, in the many industrial leagues of the day, and in the schools and colleges that competed "like the men." By the 1950s, even the female experts were split on questions of rules, interschool competition, and general emphasis. The next decades included the full flowering of interschool competition, and by the mid-1980s women had lost their autonomy. They were now, for the most part, merged under the men.[71]

Senda Berenson lived to see only some of this history. Although she continued to chair the rules committee until 1917, she retired from Smith in 1911, when she married a professor in the English department. As one biographer stated in 1941, "Mrs. Abbott felt that a full-time job was more than a faculty wife should undertake."[72] Nonetheless she and her colleagues did maintain their battle against unbridled competition, aggression, and individualism. They had seen that version of the Sportgeist and they wanted no part of it. Allen Guttmann has called this a "Canute-like effort to halt the tide of modern sports." He emphasizes their resistance to what he calls a "logic" of modern sport that included equal opportunities for high-level competition.[73] However, one can view their efforts as something quite different. They were not resisting anything that was essentially modern. They were resisting an old tide in the Sportgeist, one that could quickly flow toward aggressiveness, individualism, and the reckless pursuit of victory. This was something they feared could jeopardize their efforts to carve out a special sphere of freedom and autonomy. In this sense, they were stemming an old tide—not a new one.

CONCLUSION

Each of the individuals profiled here made significant contributions to the development of American sport. More importantly, they all forged links in a chain connecting journalists, coaches, administrators, governing bodies, and sporting goods firms. This assemblage supplied the foundation for an industry of providers, who packaged and sold sports to a public of consumers eager to buy their expertise. Each group was an instrument for developing and circulating new commodities of expertise and authority. Sport journalism was expanding on its own, with newspapers competing for bigger and better sports sections, and dime novelists churning out ever increasing numbers of athletic heroes. Guidebooks and rulebooks showered the marketplace. If they focused on one sport, they usually contained advertisements about others. For instance, Wright and Ditson published the intercollegiate football guidebook for a time in the late 1880s. In it they liberally sprinkled advertisements for their [Dickie] Sears model tennis racquet, James Dwight's instructional booklet on lawn tennis, and their battery of baseball primers, including *Base Running* by the legendary Mike "King" Kelly and *Batting* by John Morrill. All firms pushed their relationships with experts.[74]

Berenson, Sullivan, and Chadwick had a reason for forging links with a sporting goods firm like Spalding's. Sporting goods circulated widely in the marketplace as tangible and rather durable manifestations of expertise. If these people shared anything it was a Sportgeist of regimen under the management of professional experts like themselves. They sought what Burton Bledstein has called "special power over worldly experience." They enjoyed a fair amount of it, for their positioning at the crossroads of bureaucracy, technology, and information gave them what Paul Starr has called "gatekeeping" status. Whoever wanted to play the *real* game had to play under their rules, using the official equipment sanctioned by their organizations, preferably with the tactics outlined in their guidebooks.[75]

For a price, these leaders offered the public preformed packages of play, sanctioned by their expert authority. It was by most accounts a happy exchange. Even the muckrakers who exposed Spalding's "Athletic Trust" and vilified baseball's magnates had little impact on the buying public, who followed Sullivan's suggestion to leave it to the experts. As he wrote in 1901:

> From those who are not athletically inclined I have heard criticism that so much money should be spent on athletics. That is natural, but to those who have been giving up their entire time and life for the advancement of athletics in the hope of building up the future of our race, the amount spent has seemed too little. Why should not the advancement we have made in athletics receive the same recognition as the advancement we have made in science, art, and literature?[76]

Doubtless Chadwick, Spalding, and Berenson would have agreed. All desired the higher status and respectability that a new profession might yield. For the most part, their dreams were fulfilled.

At the same time, each experienced frustrations in the attempt to harness a particular vision of the Sportgeist. The public might have to work through the modern sport structure developed by experts like Chadwick, Spalding, Sullivan, and Berenson, but people did not have to reproduce the textures of competition, physicality, creativity, or achievement envisioned by those experts. Rules could be stretched. Technical advice could be used to different ends than those intended by authors. So could equipment, facilities, and bureaucracies. As it had been for millenia, the Sportgeist was nothing but a set of *potentials.* Those potentials were animated by people. If the people did not share the same life conditions, the same views of the world as the experts, there was a strong chance that they would animate alternative visions of the Sportgeist.

All the modern structures in American sport have not prevented the recurrence of those ancient tensions. Thus we find ourselves perplexed as we try to balance winning with fair play, aggressiveness with control, freedom with technique, and the individual with community. In this regard we are no more modern than the ancient Greeks. To this extent there is nothing new under the sun.

NOTES

*I wish to thank the following for assistance: Bill Deane, National Baseball Hall of Fame and Museum; Maida Goodwin, Smith College Archives; Gisela Schlüter Terrell, the Irwin Library, Butler University; Chip Powers, Amateur Athletic Union; Ronald A.

Smith; William A. Sutton; John Loy; Pat Nahin, Donna Hardy, and the librarians at the University of New Hampshire; and Gary Stark and Donald Kyle, University of Texas at Arlington.

1. Richard Mandell, *Sport: A Cultural History* (New York: Columbia University Press, 1984), xiv. For definitions of sport, see also Jay J. Coakley, *Sport and Society: Issues and Controversies*, 3rd ed. (St. Louis: Mosby, 1986); John Loy, "The Nature of Sport: A Definitional Effort," *Quest* 10 (May, 1968): 1–15; Robert W. Henderson, *Ball, Bat and Bishop: The Origin of Ball Games* (New York: Rockport Press, 1947); Allen Guttmann, *From Ritual to Record: The Nature of Modern Sports* (New York: Columbia University Press, 1978); Melvin Adelman, *A Sporting Time: New York City and the Rise of Modern Athletics* (Urbana, Ill.: University of Illinois Press, 1986). For a critique of the modernization school, see Richard Gruneau, "Modernization or Hegemony: Two Views on Sport and Social Development," in *Les Enjeux Sociaux du Sport*, ed. Jean Harvey and Hart Cantelon (Ottawa: University of Ottawa Press, 1987).

2. David Sansone, *Greek Athletics and the Genesis of Sport* (Berkeley: University of California Press, 1988), 43.

3. Ibid., 47, 62.

4. Ibid., 62–63.

5. Ibid, 50–61; Michael Salter, "Play in Ritual," in *Play and Culture*, ed. Helen B. Schwartzman (West Point, N.Y.: Leisure Press, 1979), 70–82.

6. See reviews by Allen Guttmann and Donald Kyle in *Journal of Sport History* 15 (Winter 1988): 356–62, and Jasper Griffin, "Playing to Win," *New York Review of Books*, Sept. 29, 1988, 3–5.

7. For Hegel's "Geist," see Carl J. Friedrich, ed., *The Philosophy of Hegel* (New York: Modern Library, 1953); J. N. Findlay, *Hegel: A Re-Examination* (London: Allen & Unwin, 1958); G. W. F. Hegel, *Lectures on the Philosophy of World History*, trans. from Hoffmeister edition by H. S. Nisbet (Cambridge: Cambridge University Press, 1975). My conception of the Sportgeist is influenced by the long train of materialist critiques of Hegel, begun in Karl Marx and Friedrich Engels, *The German Ideology*, ed. C. J. Arthur (New York: International Publ., 1947).

8. Homer, *Iliad* 23.439–546; Matthew W. Dickie, "Fair and Foul Play in the Funeral Games in the *Iliad*," *Journal of Sport History* 11 (Summer 1984): 8–17. I am indebted to Donald Kyle for sound advice in handling ancient subjects. Lingering errors are mine.

9. Homer, *Iliad* 23.651–669, quoted in Waldo E. Sweet, *Sport and Recreation in Ancient Greece* (New York: Oxford University Press, 1987), 21–22. For an excellent analysis of combat sports, see Michael B. Poliakoff, *Combat Sports in the Ancient World: Competition, Violence, and Culture* (New Haven: Yale University Press, 1987).

10. Homer, *Iliad* 23.733, 823, quoted in Stephen G. Miller, *Arete* (Chicago: Ares, 1979), 10.

11. Johann Huizinga, *Homo Ludens: A Study of the Play Element in Culture* (Boston: Beacon, 1955). For an elaborate treatment of freedom versus constraint in sport, see Richard Gruneau, *Class, Sport, and Social Development* (Amherst, University of Massachusetts Press, 1984).

12. Philostratus, *On Athletics*, 1–2, 44–54, quoted in Sweet, *Sport and Recreation*, 213–14, 223, 227–28.

13. Pindar, *Olympian*, 8.77, *Pythian*, 2, in *Odes in Pindar*, trans. C. M. Bowra (Baltimore: Penguin, 1969), 213, 146.

14. Thucydides, 6.16.1f., trans. Benjamin Jowett, rev. & abr. P. A. Brunt (New

York: Washington Square Press, 1962) 194–95; Isocrates, *Panegyricus* 50.43–44, quoted in Donald Kyle, *Athletics in Ancient Athens* (Leiden: E. J. Brill, 1987), 135. For an important discussion of the sport and community nexus, see Alan G. Ingham, Jeremy Howell, and Todd Schilperoort, "Professional Sports and Community: A Review and Exegesis," *Exercise and Sport Science Reviews*, 15 (1987): 427–65.

15. Fernand Braudel, *On History*, trans. Sarah Matthews (Chicago: University of Chicago Press, 1980), 32, 75, 87; Stuart Clark, "French Historians and Early Modern Popular Culture," *Past and Present* 99 (May, 1983): 62–99.

16. For discussions of sport and "structure," see Stephen Hardy and Alan G. Ingham, "Games, Structure, and Agency: Historians on the American Play Movement," *Journal of Social History* (Winter 1983): 285–301, and Alan G. Ingham and Stephen Hardy, "Sport: Structuration, Subjugation, and Hegemony," *Theory, Culture, and Society* 2 (1984): 85–103.

17. On the general features of this sport industry, see my "Entrepreneurs, Organizations, and the Sportmarketplace: Subjects in Search of Historians," *Journal of Sport History* 13 (Spring 1986): 14–33; idem, "Adopted By All the Leading Clubs; Sporting Goods and the Shaping of Leisure, 1800–1900," in *For Fun and Profit: The Transformation of Leisure into Consumption*, ed. Richard Butsch (Philadelphia: Temple University Press, in press). For important colonial antecedents, see Nancy Struna, "Sport and Society in Early America," *International Journal of the History of Sport* 5 (Dec., 1988): 292–311.

18. See, for example, Peter Levine, A. G. *Spalding and the Rise of Baseball: The Promise of American Sport* (New York: Oxford University Press, 1985); Adelman, *A Sporting Time*; Donald Mrozek, *Sport and American Mentality, 1880–1910* (Knoxville: University of Tennessee Press, 1984); John R. Betts, *America's Sporting Heritage* (Reading, Mass.: Addison-Wesley, 1974); Roy Rosenzweig, *Eight Hours for What We Will: Workers and Leisure in an Industrial City, 1870–1920* (New York: Cambridge University Press, 1983).

19. "Henry Chadwick," *Dictionary of American Biography*, vol. 3, ed. Allen Johnson, (New York: Charles Scribner's Sons, 1929), 587; Thomas S. Rice, "Henry Chadwick," *Sporting News*, May 21, 1936; *New York Times*, Apr. 21, 1908, p. 9.

20. Henry Chadwick, *The Game of Baseball: How to Learn It, How to Play It and How to Teach It* (New York, orig. publ. 1868; reprint ed. Columbia, S.C.: Camden House, 1983), 10.

21. Henry Chadwick, *The American Game of Baseball* (Philadelphia: Theodore Holland, 1889), 6; Adelman, *A Sporting Time*, 173.

22. Chadwick, *Game of Baseball*, 13; idem, *The American Game*, 34; David Voigt, *American Baseball*, 3 vols. (Norman: Oklahoma University Press, 1966), 1: 208; Adelman, *Sporting Time*, 169.

23. Henry Chadwick, "Old Time Baseball," *Outing* 39 (July, 1901): 422; Adelman, *Sporting TIme*, 166.

24. *New York Times*, Sept. 14, 1905, p. 10.

25. Voigt, *American Baseball*, 1: 6; Adelman, *Sporting Time*, 106.

26. *Sporting Life*, Apr. 27, 1887.

27. L. J. DeBekker, "The Father of the Game," *Harpers' Weekly* 51 (June 8, 1907): 838; Voigt, *American Baseball*, 1: 253.

28. Chadwick, *Game of Baseball*, 31.

29. *Sporting Goods Dealer*, Oct., 1899, p. 8; much of this section is based on my "Adopted by All the Leading Clubs."

30. Levine, *Spalding*, xiii.

31. My biographical sketch relies on Levine, *Spalding*, 3–26.

32. See Spalding's autobiographical treatise, *America's National Pastime* (New York: American Sports Publishing Co. 1911) for criticism of egotistical players and selfish interlopers.

33. Levine, *Spalding*, 71–95. Levine was the first historian to take a serious look at sporting goods. For Spalding's competition see my "Adopted by All the Leading Clubs."

34. *Sporting News*, May 13 and 27, 1893.

35. Levine, *Spalding*, 82.

36. *Sporting News*, Feb. 23, 1889.

37. Assorted football rule books and guidebooks, 1876–91, in Box 41, folders 149–50, Walter Camp Papers, Manuscripts and Archives, Yale University Library, hereafter cited as "Walter Camp Papers, YUL." The definitive work on early college sports is Ronald A. Smith, *Sports and Freedom: The Rise of Big-Time College Athletics* (New York: Oxford University Press, 1988).

38. Football rules for 1892, Box 41, folder 149; Julian Curtiss to Walter Camp, Apr. 25, 1902, Box 23, folder 641, Walter Camp Papers, YUL.

39. Walter Camp, *Walter Camp's Book of College Sports* (New York: The Century Co., 1895) 114.

40. "James E. Sullivan," *Dictionary of American Biography*, vol. 18, ed. Dumas Malone (New York: Charles Scribner's Sons, 1936) 118–19.

41. Ibid.; *National Cyclopaedia of American Biography*, vol. 15 (New York: James T. White, 1916), 54; *New York Times*, Sept. 17, 1914, p. 9; Levine, *Spalding*, 82ff; John A. Lucas, "Early Olympic Antagonists: Pierre de Coubertin versus James E. Sullivan," *Stadion* 3 no. 2 (1977): 258–72.

42. Lucas, "Early Olympic Antagonists," 263; *New York Times*, Jan. 22, Sept. 24, 1888, Feb. 24, 1891; Robert Korsgaard, "A History of the Amateur Athletic Union of the United States," (D.Ed. diss., Columbia University, 1952); Arnold Flath, "A History of Relations Between the National Collegiate Athletic Association and the Amateur Athletic Union," (Ph.D. diss., University of Michigan, 1963); Ted Vincent, *Mudville's Revenge: The Rise and Fall of American Sport* (New York: Seaview Books, 1981), 30–86.

43. James E. Sullivan, *An Athletic Primer. How to Organize a Club* (New York: American Sports Publishing Co., 1902), 21. For a strong account of sports and the fears of racial depletion, see Mrozek, *Sport and American Mentality*, 3–27.

44. Lucas, "Early Antagonists," 260; James E. Sullivan, "Athletics and the Stadium," *Cosmopolitan* 31 (Sept., 1901): 502, 505; *New York Times*, Feb. 20, 1907.

45. Sullivan, *Primer*, 11, 23, 78, 120; *Spirit of the Times* Apr. 7, 1888.

46. *New York Times*, Dec. 22, 1906, p. 7; Jan. 1, 1907, p. 10.

47. James E. Sullivan, "What Happened at Stockholm," *Outing* 61 (Oct., 1912): 31. Sullivan to Walter Camp, July 27, 1894, Box 2, folder 38, Walter Camp Papers, YUL.

48. Korsgaard, "History of AAU," 221–22, 236–37.

49. Sullivan to Camp, Nov. 30, 1896, Dec. 11, 1900, Box 2, folder 38; Sullivan to Julian Curtiss, Jan. 9, 1908, Box 2, folder 42, Walter Camp Papers, YUL.

50. *New York Times*, Dec. 5, 1909, sec. 4, p. 1.

51. *New York Times*, July 26, 1908, sec. 4, p. 1; Aug. 8, 1908, p. 6.

52. Quoted in Lucas, "Early Antagonists," p. 269.

53. "The Two Athletic Standards," *Nation*, 95 (Aug. 22, 1912): 163.

54. Thorpe's Disqualification," *Literary Digest* 46 (Feb. 8, 1913): 304.

55. See Lucas, "Early Antagonists" for details.

56. *New York Times,* Sept. 29, 1910.

57. Cindy Himes, "The Female Athlete in American Society, 1860–1940," (Ph.D. diss., University of Pennsylvania, 1986), 64. See also Roberta J. Park, "Sport Gender and Society in a Transatlantic Perspective," in *From Fair Sex to Feminism: Sport and the Socialization of Women in the Industrial and Post Industrial Eras,* ed. J. A. Mangan and Roberta J. Park (London: Frank Cass, 1987), 58–93; Betty Spears, "The Influential Miss Homans," *Quest* 29 (Winter 1979): 46–57.

58. Lucille Eaton Hill, ed., *Athletics and Outdoor Sports for Women* (New York: Macmillan, 1903), 4.

59. Himes, "Female Athlete," 95.

60. Her father's name was Valvrojenski. See Ronald A. Smith, "Senda Berenson," *Dictionary of American Biography,* Supplement Five, 1951–55, ed. John Garraty (New York: Charles Scribner's Sons, 1977), 51–52; Agnes C. R. Stillman, "Senda Berenson Abbott: Her Life and Contributions to Smith College, and to the Physical Education Profession," (M.S. thesis, Smith College, 1971).

61. Edith Naomi Hill, "Senda Berenson," in *Pioneers in Physical Education,* Supplement to *Research Quarterly,* 12, (Oct., 1944), 661. Photos in Senda Berenson Papers, Smith College Archives, hereafter cited as "Senda Berenson Papers, SCA."

62. Lecture Notes, in Senda Berenson Papers, SCA; Senda Berenson, "The Significance of Basket Ball for Women," in *Basket Ball for Women,* ed. Senda Berenson (New York; American Sports Publishing Co., 1903), p. 33.

63. Senda Berenson letter to Moses True, Dec. 11, 1906; Lecture Notes; "Athletics for Women" in Speech Notes, Senda Berenson Papers, SCA.

64. "Editorial," *Basket Ball for Women,* p. 7.

65. Rule II, Rule III, "Significance," p. 37 in *Basket Ball for Women.*

66. Ibid; Hill, "Senda Berenson," 663; "Teachers of Physical Education," in Speech Notes, Senda Berenson Papers, SCA.

67. Berenson, Lecture Notes, Senda Berenson Papers, SCA; unidentified news clippings, 1895, in Student Athletics—Basketball Files, Smith College Archives.

68. Linda Kerber, "Separate Spheres, Female Worlds, Woman's Place: The Rhetoric of Women's History," *Journal of American History* 75 (June 1988): 32. This article is an excellent review of "separate spheres"—in history and in historiography.

69. *New York Times,* Mar. 23, 1896, p. 3; Elizabeth Paine, "Physical Training in Women's Colleges—Smith," *Illustrated Sporting News,* June 4, 1904, pp. 3–4, 17; 1893 news clipping in Student Athletics–Basketball Files, Smith College Archives.

70. Report of 1895 and photos of lines: Student Athletics—Basketball Files, Smith College Archives. *New York Times,* Mar. 23, 1896, p. 3.

71. The history of control in women's athletics is clearly detailed in Joan Hult, "The Governance of Athletics For Girls and Women: Leadership by Women Physical Educators, 1899–1949," *Research Quarterly for Exercise and Sport* (Centennial Issue, 1985): 164–77. See also, Himes, "The Female Athlete," and Ronald Smith, "The Rise of Basketball for Women in Colleges," *Canadian Journal of History of Sport and Physical Education* 1 (Dec. 1970); 18–36.

72. Hill, "Senda Berenson," 665.

73. Allen Guttmann, *A Whole New Ball Game: An Interpretation of American Sports* (Chapel Hill: University of North Carolina Press, 1988), 149.

74. Rule books for 1887 and 1888 in Box 41, folder 150, Walter Camp Papers, YUL.

75. Thomas Haskell, ed., *The Authority of Experts* (Bloomington: Indiana University Press, 1984). For more on this relationship see my "Adopted by All the Leading

Clubs." See also Mrozek, *Sport and American Mentality*, 86–91. Burton Bledstein, *The Culture of Professionalism: The Middle Class and the Development of Higher Education* (New York: Norton, 1976), 90. Paul Starr, *The Social Transformation of American Medicine* (New York: Basic Books, 1982), 15, 22.

76. Sullivan, "Athletics and the Stadium," 508. For a classic but ineffectual muckraking piece, see James B. Connolly, "The Capitalization of Amateur Athletics," *Metropolitan Magazine*, July, 1910, 443–54.

STEVEN A. RIESS

Professional Sports as an Avenue of Social Mobility in America: Some Myths and Realities

ONE OF the most important traditional American beliefs has long been the concept of social mobility. In only a few other western societies has the general public been so convinced that widespread opportunities existed for individuals to rise above their socioeconomic origins through their own skills, hard work, and good fortune. Americans and foreigners alike have believed that ambitious people could succeed in the United States because it was achievement, and not parentage, that counted in our meritocratic society. People got ahead in the era of industrial capitalism by becoming well educated, making valuable social contacts, employing scarce familial resources to start a business, and by growing up in homes where values relevant to a modernized urban society, such as deferred gratification, were taught. Deprived youths lacking these advantages were not completely blocked from advancement because they could rely on alternative routes to success. Instead of becoming professionals or entrepreneurs, they might get involved in such activities as religion, politics, crime, and entertainment. These occupations required a lot of talent and drive, and they were not all respectable or even legitimate.[1]

Ever since the rise of professional sports in the mid-nineteenth century, the general public and opinion makers have regarded sport as an alternate means of vertical mobility because it was a democratic institution in which participants rose or fell solely on the basis of talent, training, and perseverance. Everyone "knew" that prize fighters came from impoverished rough inner city neighborhoods; that basketball players were either tough slum kids or hot shooting Indiana farm boys; that baseball players were somewhat better off small town boys who wanted something better than farm or factory work; and that football players were second-generation Ohioans and Pennsylvanians hoping to escape the steel mills and coal mines where their fathers worked.[2]

These popular conceptions were generally accepted until the early 1970s when social activists, sociologists, and sporting figures whose consciousness had been raised by the athletic revolution of the late 1960s began questioning the assumption that professional sport was a significant vehicle for social mobility. Social activists and sociologists, such as Harry Edwards, and sports stars, such as Arthur Ashe and Walt Frazier, became concerned that black teenagers were devoting too much time to sports, which the youth perceived as a ticket out of the ghetto, instead of to education. These critics pointed out that there was very little chance of using sport as an escape because of the limited number of jobs in professional sports and the brief tenure of professional athletes. In baseball, for instance, back in 1910 there were only 240 positions in the major leagues, and just 624 even in 1988. A 1972 study found that a high school baseball player had a one in four thousand chance of becoming a big leaguer; in football, the odds were one in 3,750 of making the National Football League (NFL); and one in ten thousand of making the National Basketball Association (NBA). Furthermore, even if a poor kid made it successfully into professional sports, that mobility would be likely to be temporary because of the severe problems many former athletes faced in their second careers after sports.[3]

Historians have virtually neglected to analyze whether or not professional sport has been a significant means of social advancement for youth with limited options, despite the work of Stephen Thernstrom and others on American social mobility and the recent boom in sport history.[4] This essay seeks to fill that gap in the literature, assessing the value of professional sport as a source of social mobility in the United States by examining the social, ethnic, and geographic origins, and the subsequent employment history, of men who participated in prize fighting, major league baseball, professional football, and professional basketball from the earliest days of those sports up to 1980. While there have always been sufficient rags to riches stories to perpetuate the popular belief that sport was an important alternate means of social advancement, I will argue, along with the contemporary social critics, that sport is overrated as a means of upward mobility. Most of the professional athletes examined did not make a lot of money, had short careers, and ended up in occupations that normally had more to do with their social origins and level of education than their athletic fame.

PRIZE FIGHTING

Boxing was one of the first professional sports in America. By the 1840s illegal contests were fought by professionals for sidebets in cities including New York, Boston, Baltimore, Philadelphia, and New Orleans. Such cities all had large communities of traditionally oriented, lower-class immigrants who provided most fighters and spectators. In New York, the center of antebellum pugilism, more than half (56.3 percent) of the fighters active between 1840 and 1860 were Irish-born; one-sixth (15.6 percent) were second-generation Irish; and one-fifth (18.8 percent) were English-born. Many of the foreign-born boxers had been professional fighters prior to immigrating. The native-born were the product of street gangs or volunteer fire companies, and were either unskilled or semiskilled workers. These poor urbanites fought infrequently and depended for employment on political sponsors for whom they became "shoulder hitters" (political intimidators) during elections. They frequently held patronage jobs, often in the police department, or worked as immigrant runners (recruiters of immigrants for jobs), saloon managers, or bouncers.[5]

Few early prize fighters made a lot of money. John Morrissey, an Irish-American who was national champion from 1853 to 1858, was a rare exception. Active in Tammany politics, Morrissey used his fame and charisma among fellow Irish-Americans to get elected to the U.S. Congress in 1866. He became rich through the gambling business, operating the leading betting parlor in New York City, and played a prominent role in the development of Saratoga Springs into an elite resort by establishing a casino and racetrack there during the Civil War.[6]

Boxing continued to struggle after the Civil War, and matches had to be held in out-of-the-way places like barns, barges, and saloon backrooms to evade the arm of the law. It was difficult for pugilists to develop a career until the late nineteenth century when the sport was given a great boost by the arrival of a charismatic world heavyweight champion, John L. Sullivan (1882–92), and the growing popularity of the *National Police Gazette*, which every week vividly reported the events of the boxing world to its legions of readers. Sullivan, the greatest sport hero of the century, earned more than half a million dollars during his career even though his matches were nearly always illegal, and defenses had to be held in such remote sites as Richburg, Mississippi. His exploits were widely followed in the daily press and Richard K. Fox's *National Police Gazette*, which had a circulation of about 150,000. Well-worn copies of the pink periodical could be found in many an American saloon, barber shop, and billiard parlor, and in other bastions of male subculture.[7]

In the 1890s prize fighting was temporarily permitted for the first time in New Orleans and New York, and police often looked the other way when major matches were held in Chicago, Denver, and San Francisco. Championship bouts were arranged for purses of up to forty thousand dollars plus sidebets of as high as ten thousand dollars. Champions and contenders became role models for inner city youth, for whom boxing fit in well with their environment. Boys and young men from different ethnic backgrounds were frequently getting into brawls to protect their turf, themselves, or the honor of their ethnic group. There were many opportunities to learn the "manly art" at neighborhood settlement houses and local gymnasiums, and it helped boys defend themselves and build up their self-confidence. The ability to fight well in the gym and back on the streets enabled slum youth to prove their manliness, gain respect from their peers, and secure training for a future career as either a prize fighter or a hoodlum.[8]

Professional boxers were drawn almost exclusively from impoverished urban slum backgrounds. The sport required intensive training to build up strength, endurance, and the ability to withstand physical punishment. Few people with alternative opportunities would choose to get their skulls smashed in for a few dollars and the aspiration of becoming a contender. The sport continued to be thoroughly dominated by the Irish until the 1920s. In the nineteenth century the Irish were always among the poorest immigrants. About ninety percent of first-generation Irishmen were blue-collar, overwhelmingly unskilled workers, and social mobility was difficult for their poorly educated sons growing up in rough neighborhoods like New York's Hell's Kitchen. Such communities were the breeding grounds of future prize fighters. In the 1890s, nine of the nineteen world champions were Irish-Americans, and men like Jack Dempsey, "the Nonpareil," James Corbett, and John L. Sullivan were role models for Irish youth. Between 1900 and 1920 there were more Irish champions (thirteen out of forty-seven) and contenders (forty percent in 1909 and 1916) than men from any other ethnic group. Irish fighters continued to be successful for many years, but their dominance gradually declined because of improved opportunities in business and politics as the Irish became more established, and because of increasingly stiff competition in the ring from other impoverished, second-generation immigrants.[9]

Sons of eastern and southern European immigrants achieved great success in boxing more rapidly than in any other major sport. Like the Irish before them, they were tough inner city kids, typically ex-street fighters whose idols were either boxers or gangsters, the only well-paying occupations that seemed open to them. Boxing suited the living conditions of these immigrants, and unlike other sports including baseball, boxing also provided opportunities for men of slight stature to compete in different weight divisions. By 1901 there were already two Jewish world champions, including featherweight Abe Atell who held his crown until 1912. In the teens of the century more champions were Jewish than from any other ethnic group except the Irish. By 1908 there was a Polish titleholder, middleweight Stanley Ketchell, and an Italian champion, bantamweight Pete Herman, was crowned in 1917. It would be over twenty years before either of these two immigrant groups would have a major league batting champion, yet the Italians were already third in the number of boxing contenders, behind the Irish and the Germans. During the 1920s there were more Jewish contenders than men from any other group; ten years later the Italians were the leaders. From 1920 until 1939 there were a total of twenty-four Italian-American and fifteen Jewish-American world champions.[10]

Black fighters also had opportunities in the squared circle. At the turn of the century when black professional athletes were being forced out of horse racing, cycling, and organized baseball, blacks were achieving considerable renown in boxing. Between 1890 and 1908 there were five black world champions, although many leading contenders could not even get a title match because champions like John L. Sullivan drew the color line. Furthermore, interracial bouts were widely prohibited. After the riots that followed the 1910 Johnson-Jeffries heavyweight championship bout, the ban spread and even included New York, the capital of American boxing.[11]

Boxing over the next several decades continued to attract black interest because it was the only professional sport open to black athletes. During the Great Depression 22.5 percent of the approximately eight thousand professional American boxers were black. Like their white peers, they were attracted by the opportunity to make a living, escape their slum origins, and gain a measure of fame and possible wealth. There were five black world champions in the 1930s, including Henry Armstrong, the first man to win three different titles, and Joe Louis, heavyweight champion from 1937 to 1949. The first black fighter to get a crack at the heavyweight crown since Jack Johnson, Louis represented the "ideal negro" to whites, but at the same time he symbolized racial pride, black power, and an insistence that blacks be accepted in American society. He was a role model for young blacks like Malcolm Little (Malcolm X), and a knight errant to blacks from all social backgrounds.[12]

Soon after the depression blacks dominated prize fighting. By 1948 nearly half of all contenders were black, reflecting widespread black poverty, limited avenues of upward mobility, and role models like Joe Louis. Italians were second and Mexican-Americans third in producing contenders. Black preeminence had become even stronger by 1980, with Latins a distant second. These fighters were virtually all from lower-class origins. A study by sociologist S. Kirson Weinberg of sixty-eight fighters active in the 1940s found that just two were middle-class. These boxers were mainly newcomers to the city or else children of immigrants who resided in the poorest sections of town. They were usually former street gang members who had been influenced by a local idol or an older relative who had boxed. Sociologist Nathan Hare studied the family backgrounds of a sample of predominantly black Chicago pugilists active in the 1960s and found that just one-third (35 percent) had working fathers at home; they were virtually all working-class. Almost as many fathers (29 percent) had deserted their families as were employed.[13]

The recruitment pattern in prize fighting was a prime example of ethnic succession and reflected the changing composition of inner cities that were the chief sources of boxers. When longer established ethnic groups which had dominated pugilism began doing better economically and moved out of urban slums, they were replaced by newer arrivals in the inner city, who would also follow them into the prize ring. For example, before World War II, Jews were a prominent group inside the ring, but as they became better educated or succeeded in business, they moved out of neighborhoods like the Lower East Side of New York to better areas. The result was that their sons did not need to get their heads bashed in to make a living, and the Jewish boxing champion became a rarity.

The top prize fighters made huge amounts of money, and in every era have been the most highly compensated athletes. In 1910, for instance, Jack Johnson got one hundred thousand dollars for his successful defense against Jim Jeffries. Seventeen years later Gene Tunney was paid $990,000 when he defended his crown against former champion Jack Dempsey in the famous "long count" fight. However, very few fighters made the big money, and most did not make much money at all. A study of 127 boxers active between 1938 and 1951 found that just 7.1 percent achieved national recognition, 8.7 percent became local headliners, and the great preponderance (84.2 percent) never advanced beyond semi-windup or preliminary matches. During the depression when there were probably more professional boxers than in any other era, hungry men fought for as little as ten dollars. Even when top contenders and champions fought for large purses, their actual take-home pay was far less because they had training expenses and usually had to pay a manager one-third off the top. Fighters with crooked managers were forced to pay even more. In 1948 lightweight champion Ike Williams earned a total of sixty-five thousand dollars for two title defenses, but ended up with nothing. His manager, Blinky Palermo, took it all. Palermo was the numbers king of Philadelphia and was associated with the infamous Frankie Carbo, the "Mr. Big" of prize fighting. Big earnings also went quickly because of fast living, large retinues, and gambling. Barney Ross, for instance, earned four hundred thousand dollars in the depression as lightweight and welterweight champion, but squandered it all. One of the saddest cases was Joe Louis, who made millions but ended up a greeter in Las Vegas, in debt to the IRS.[14]

Retired boxers fared far worse than other professional athletes. They had come from very poor backgrounds, and when in the money, allowed the cash to flow freely. They did not understand the need to save, and most did not make big money anyway. Most boxers left the ring ill-prepared for the future. They had saved little, were uneducated, had few marketable skills, and were usually (60 percent) at least mildly punch-drunk. A 1930 *Ring* magazine survey of retired boxers tried to put the sport in a favorable light by listing nearly seventy ex-fighters who were well-off, but it also named over seventy who were broke. More recently, a study of forty-eight Chicago ex-club fighters conducted in the late 1960s by Hare found that none had saved most of his purses, and one-fourth had saved nothing.[15]

What happened to the ex-fighter? A survey of 154 notable boxers active between 1900 and 1960 found that one-third (32 percent) ended up with blue-collar jobs and the rest had low level white-collar jobs. One-sixth (17 percent) were able to remain in the sport in some capacity and thereby take advantage of the one skill they had. Race and ethnicity were probably important factors. Black fighters had substantially fewer opportunities than white boxers, while Jewish fighters fared far better than their gentile peers. Out of a sample of thirty-six Jewish pugilists, I found just one who ended up with a manual job. Most of these retirees had modest nonmanual jobs, but one-third ended up as businessmen or with high white-collar jobs. A quarter (27.8 percent)—significantly more than among other ex-pugilists—remained in the sport in some capacity, often in leadership positions such as trainers and managers. The prominence of Jews in the business of boxing, especially from the 1930s up to the present day, reflects the Jewish entrepreneurial tradition.[16]

The best study of the retirement patterns of boxers is still Weinberg's "The Occupational Culture of the Boxer" (1952), which examined the retirement occupations of ninety-five former contenders and champions active in the 1940s who had earned at least one hundred thousand dollars during their careers. A quarter (25.3 percent) ended up with blue-collar jobs; another quarter (27.3 percent) owned, "fronted," or worked in a tavern; one-fifth (18.9 percent) became trainers or managers; and one-ninth (11.7 percent) entered the entertainment field. Former fighters were probably more dependent on their fame and personality in their second careers than other athletes. Hence club fighters who had no reputations to rely upon had particularly hard times after boxing and ended up about where they had started (and, at least physically, far worse off). In the 1960s only three-fourths (77.1 percent) of Chicago's former club fighters even held steady jobs after leaving the ring, and these were mainly semiskilled or unskilled jobs.[17] Boxing was a cruel sport characterized by shattered bodies, broken dreams, and hopeless futures. The fame, glamor, and mobility it provided, if any, were fleeting. Even champions ended up blind, mentally impaired, and destitute; and a job might be nothing more than shining shoes or selling neckties on the streets of Miami.

PROFESSIONAL BASKETBALL

Invented in 1891 by Dr. James Naismith to provide football players with wintertime exercise, basketball quickly became popular in inner city neighborhoods because it was a cheap sport that did not require much space. By the mid-1890s basketball was being played in YMCAs, settlement houses, church facilities, and schools. The first professional league was established in 1898 in Philadelphia. Over the next few years inner city settlement houses became the principal breeding grounds for future interscholastic, collegiate, and professional stars who were mainly drawn from the poorer ethnic groups. In 1912 a club called the Celtics was established at the Hudson Guild, a New York settlement house located in a predominantly Irish neighborhood, and it became the leading professional team of the 1920s. Star Celtics players earned about twelve thousand dollars a year, far more than any other basketball players of their era. They played hundreds of games each year, often against semiprofessional clubs. The best semipro players usually got twenty-five dollars a game, but against the Celtics their pay might be tripled. In 1923 the Celtics were 193–11, usually going easy on opponents, instead of running up the score, in order to build up interest in a return engagement and to encourage betting. The premier teams of the 1920s were ethnically-oriented, independent touring clubs like the Celtics, the Philadelphia SPHAs (South Philadelphia Hebrew Association), and the Harlem Rens.[18]

The first national professional basketball association was the American Basketball League (1926–31), a modestly financed operation with franchises in several major markets. Limited press coverage, unbalanced competition, the absence of certain top teams like the all-black Rens, and the coming of the depression did in the league. In the 1930s professional basketball was a minor sport. There were, in addition to touring teams like the Rens and the Harlem Globetrotters, two weekend leagues, the American Basketball League (1934) in the East and the National Basketball League (NBL—1937) in the Midwest. Players in these leagues were not full-time athletes but participated to earn a second income. Many top players chose to forego professional basketball rather than lose their amateur standing unless sufficiently compensated. In 1940, for example, the Chicago Bruins offered Santa Clara All-American Ralph Gianinni two hundred dollars a month plus a job at a local racetrack, but he felt the compensation was inadequate to move halfway across the country, and he turned them down.[19]

Basketball became fully professionalized only after World War II. In 1946 eleven businessmen who controlled the best eastern and midwestern indoor arenas established the Basketball Association of America (BAA) to complement their other attractions, and in 1949 this merged with the NBL to form the National Basketball Association. Salaries at the time were modest. Top players in the NBL earned up to $12,000 a year, which was double the maximum paid by the BAA. Salaries rose moderately over the next twenty years, reaching an average of $25,000 in 1967, only to jump sixty percent to $40,000 in 1971 because of competition from the new American Basketball Association. Since then salaries have continued to escalate rapidly, mainly due to the elimination of the reserve clause. The average salary surpassed six figures by 1975, reaching $185,000 by 1980 and $300,000 by 1984. Basketball players had become the most highly paid team athletes.[20]

Little is known about professional basketball players who were active before 1940, although they were probably mainly urban white ethnics from lower-class origins. Of a sample of forty-four American-born oldtimers drawn from Ronald L. Mendell's *Who's Who in Basketball*, over ninety percent came from cities, with a majority (51.2 percent) from metropolitan New York. Three-fourths of them were German, Jewish, or Irish. Many had developed their skills in community or settlement house leagues—college basketball did not become a big time sport until the 1930s—yet three-quarters (74.4 percent) of these professionals had attended college. This rate of attendance far exceeded the national norm (in 1939–40, 15.3 percent of college age youth were in school), a particularly notable statistic since the early pros were mainly from lower-class backgrounds. Basketball scholarships provided indigent youth with a means to attend college. The pro basketball pioneers did exceptionally well after leaving the sport: nearly all (95.1 percent) ended up with white-collar jobs. Over three-fifths (61 percent) secured high level white-collar jobs as attorneys, teachers, and other professionals.

These athletes recognized the limitations of touring or weekend competition, and were well prepared for the future. Poor inner city kids who became basketball players fared far better over the long haul than their neighbors who had become prize fighters.[21]

A second sample of professional basketball players includes 218 men who were born before 1940 and played professionally after World War II. They were mainly National Basketball Association (NBA) players active in the 1950s when the sport was still a relatively modest operation (for example, in 1963 the Philadelphia Warriors club was sold for merely $850,000), and one hundred thousand-dollar salaries were unheard of. These men were primarily white (84.1 percent), the NBA having integrated in 1950, and probably more WASPish than in the past. Players were still predominantly urban (79.3 percent), but less so than before. Nearly half were from cities with over one hundred thousand inhabitants (45.9 percent), including better than one-fifth (22.3 percent) from major cities with over one million residents; but they were no longer as concentrated in metropolitan New York. We do not have data on the social origins of these athletes, but fragmentary data on star players of this era indicates that nearly one-fifth (18.75 percent), and probably more, came from middle-class origins. They were

Table 1
Occupations of Retired Professional Basketball Players
Born Before 1940 and Active After 1947

Occupational Category	Number	Percentage
High white-collar		
Professionals	32	16.6
Managers, high officials, and		
major proprietors	33	17.1
Subtotal	65	33.7
Low white-collar		
Clerks, sales, and kindred workers	31	16.1
Semiprofessionals	60	31.1
Petty proprietors, managers, and		
low officials	33	17.1
Subtotal	124	64.2[a]
Total white-collar	189	97.9
Blue-collar	4	2.1
Grand total	193	100.0

Source: Computed from data in Ronald L. Mendell, *Who's Who in Basketball* (New Rochelle, N.Y.: Arlington House, 1973).
[a] Error due to rounding

extremely well educated, and every player but one (Al Cervi, who left school to work in the family business) attended college. Their rate of graduation is unknown, but considering the average salaries of the era, their success after basketball, and the graduation rates of contemporary pro football players (see below), it seems likely that the graduation rate exceeded the fifty-five percent for NBA players active in the mid-1970s.[22]

The pro basketball players active in the late 1940s and 1950s fared exceptionally well in their second careers. (see table 1). Virtually all (97.9 percent) ended up with white-collar jobs, with one-third (33.7 percent) having high white-collar situations, equally divided between professionals and major businessmen. This record of achievement was a consequence of both their athletic fame and high level of education. Nearly two-fifths of their major business ventures (39.4 percent) were in sports, especially professional basketball. Of those with low white-collar jobs, a quarter (24.4 percent) became basketball coaches, mainly at the collegiate and professional levels. Other low white-collar categories included salesmen, real estate agents, insurance agents, and broadcasters; such jobs, for which fame provided an entree, comprised one-fifth (19.0 percent) of the retirement positions.

Virtually all players active in the NBA in the 1960s and 1970s who were born between 1941 and 1952 were American-born (99.5 percent), and they were overwhelmingly urban (91.2 percent) in origin. This group of players was more urban than the preceding generation of NBA players, and a little more likely to come from cities with more than one hundred thousand inhabitants (49.5 percent). The NBA recruited its players from the ranks of intercollegiate stars who mainly came from major cities. Of the 525 All-American players between 1946 and 1983, two-thirds (66.5 percent) came from the fifty-eight metropolitan areas with at least half a million residents, even though these cities comprised only half of the national population. New York was the most productive city by a wide margin (15 percent), followed by Chicago (6.3 percent), and Philadelphia and Los Angeles (3.8 percent each).[23] These gifted superstars survived the fierce competition in city leagues and had developed their skills through long hours of practice; they were motivated by the gratification of immediate prestige at neighborhood playgrounds and the long-term goals of a high school letter, a college scholarship, and eventually a spot in the NBA, and escape from poverty. By 1980, seventy-five percent of NBA players were black athletes, and basketball was the team sport most dominated by blacks. Their success has been the product of talent, hard work, and the emulation of positive role models, which have been all too lacking in urban ghettoes.[24]

The young men who make the NBA earn a minimum of $100,000, with top stars making millions of dollars a year. However, only about sixty rookies make the NBA each year, their average tenure is just 3.2 years, and most NBA aspirants complete their college eligibility without a degree or marketable skills. Only about one-third of current NBA players will ever get a degree. It remains to be seen whether active players will save for the future and/or successfully employ their fame in future occupations, or end up as a janitor, like former college scoring champion Billy "The Hill" McGill; unemployed at forty, like Dave "The Rave" Stallworth of the championship New York Knickerbockers team of 1970–71; or on drugs, as has befallen several NBA players. On a more positive note, unlike baseball or football, pro basketball has transcended racial prejudice by opening up many head coaching and executive positions.[25]

PROFESSIONAL FOOTBALL

The first paid football player was Pudge Heffelfinger, a former Yale All-American, who in 1892 was paid five hundred dollars to play for the Allegheny Athletic Association (AAA) in a game against the Pittsburgh Athletic Club. One year later the AAA paid three men fifty dollars a game each, and by 1895 all its players were on salary. Pittsburgh remained the chief locus of the professional game until 1903 when semi-pro teams in industrial Ohio cities like Canton began recruiting ex-collegians or active college men who played under a pseudonym for fifty dollars a game. Many of their teammates, and several entire teams, were made up of local manual workers, like the Columbus Panhandles, a well-known club of the next decade comprised of Pennsylvania Railroad mechanics.[26]

In 1920 the first professional league, the American Professional Football Association, was organized; two years later it became known as the National Football League (NFL). The association was originally a midwestern organization with franchises sponsored by local boosters or industrialists who employed the sport as part of their welfare capitalism program. The pro game had little prestige, drew small crowds, and was regarded as inferior to the college game. The average professional in the fledgling NFL made only $100 to $150 a game, using it as a part-time job to supplement his principal vocation. Only the handful of players who were great draws were well paid, most notably Red Grange, the former star halfback of the University of Illinois and greatest collegiate player of the 1920s. His income with the Chicago Bears was tied to gate receipts, and he earned about $250,000 in his rookie year, mostly from the team's two national tours, which drew enormous crowds and set records in every stadium.[27]

Grange's presence in the NFL began to turn things around for the sport. In the 1930s pro football was a full-time job, and the league was becoming stabilized. By 1934 all the small town franchises like Pottsville had been eliminated (with the exception of Green Bay), and replaced by teams in major eastern and midwestern markets. Most former collegiate stars were now dotting NFL rosters because of the improved status of the pro game, higher salaries, and opportunity to postpone adulthood; possible off-season job opportunities; and the possibilities of enhancing future career prospects by earning money to pay for additional education, or making good connections and gaining experience to prepare them for a coaching career. Top salaries during the 1930s ranged from about $3,600 to $6,000 a year, topped by Rhodes Scholar rookie Byron "Whizzer" White's $15,000 in 1938. Most players, however, earned considerably less, probably closer to $150 a game, but they supplemented this with off-season jobs, making them quite well-off during the depression.[28]

After World War II, professional football enjoyed a small boom, resulting in the emergence of a rival league, the All-American Conference. A bidding war for players followed, pushing up the average NFL salary to $8,000 in 1949. Over the next decade salaries rose modestly to a mean of $9,200, not even keeping up with inflation. However, the rise of the American Football League in 1960 drastically changed the salary structure; the competition for players propelled the average wage up to $25,000 in 1967. By 1975 the average was up to $42,000, but it began to lag behind baseball and basketball, which had achieved free agency. Still, NFL average salaries continued to rise very significantly, reaching $69,000 in 1980 and $254,000 in 1988.[29]

In its semipro era and in the first years of NFL pro football, with its low prestige and meager salaries, this was a very democratic sport, open to all ethnic groups. Blacks played in the NFL until 1934 when they were barred by common consent, and there was even an all-Indian team, the Oorong Indians, a touring squad ostensibly based in Marion, Ohio, from 1922 to 1924. Yet probably ninety percent of the players were native-born or of German, Irish, or other old immigrant stock. A substantial proportion of semipro and early NFL players were blue-collar workers employed in factories that sponsored professional elevens. This was reflected by the relatively large segment of players active in the NFL between 1920 and 1932 who had not attended college (18.7 percent). The non-college NFL players were concentrated in the period before 1926 (81.7 percent) when the NFL was struggling to survive and was having a hard time recruiting intercollegiate stars.[30]

A significant shift in recruitment patterns occurred towards the end of the 1920s with the decline of the non-college men. Between 1932 and 1945, ninety-eight percent of NFL players had attended college. College football players had always been recognized as the top players, and once the idea of playing professional football became socially acceptable and economically rewarding, the college gridiron became the equivalent of the minor leagues for organized baseball. NFL players were far more likely to have attended college compared to major league baseball players (20 percent in 1941), or even the pioneer pro basketball players (74.4 percent). Furthermore, they were among the best educated men in the United States. Not only did they virtually all attend college, but 85.5 percent had degrees and 31.3 percent had advanced degrees. They were true scholar-athletes.[31]

The high educational achievements of these players reflected their social backgrounds (see table 2). Most of them came from the "football belt" but were not, as stereotypes would have it, sons of factory workers or miners employing sports as an alternate avenue of social mobility. Players active in the 1930s came from families that economically and socially were distinctly middle-class. Almost six out of ten (57.8 percent) had white-collar fathers and just one out of three (33.3 percent) had blue-collar fathers. Even though nearly half (45.2 percent) of the players had been born in rural areas, only 8.9 percent were sons of farmers. Futhermore, the fathers were mainly employed in high white-collar or skilled blue-collar jobs. Two-thirds (64.3 percent) of the

Table 2
Occupations of Fathers of NFL Players
Active 1920–1980s

Occupational Category	1920s–40s[a] n = 66 (%)	1930s[b] n = 45 (%)	1949[c] n = 300 (%)	1950s[b] n = 111 (%)	1950s–80s[a] n = 124 (%)	1969–80[d] n = 87[f] (%)
White-collar	53.0	57.8	46.6[f]	40.5	40.3	47.1
Blue-collar	33.3	33.3	45.5[f]	52.2	53.2	52.9[g]
Farmer	13.6	8.9	7.9[f]	7.2	6.5	0
Grand total	99.99[e]	100.0	100.0	99.9[e]	100.0	100.0
	***	**	***	***	***	

[a] Data from David L. Porter, ed., *Biographical Dictionary of American Sports*, vol. 2, *Football* (Westport, Conn.: Greenwood Press, 1987).
[b] Study data collected by Riess.
[c] Data from Paul Governali, "The Professional Football Player: His Vocational Status" (M.A. thesis, Teachers' College, Columbia University, 1951), 49.
[d] Data from Larry Van Roe, "A Descriptive Study of the Effects of Career Termination upon Journeyman Professional Football Players (Ed.D. diss., University of Georgia, 1984), 135.
[e] Error due to rounding
[f] Adjusted to discount for no data responses
[g] Includes foremen
**p < .01
***p < .001

manual fathers were artisans; just one out of sixteen (6.3 percent) was a miner. The high status of the players was indicated by their marital partners. Nearly two-thirds of players active in the 1930s (64.5 percent) had college-educated wives at a time when few Americans attended college, and almost half were college graduates. Over three-fifths of these spouses (63.6 percent) had white-collar fathers, with the remainder evenly divided up between blue-collar and farmer fathers. Clearly, these athletes were good catches.[32]

Middle-class dominance in pro football was short-lived because the sport became increasingly accessible to upwardly mobile athletes who used their prowess first to secure a scholarship, and then continued to a professional football career. Sociologist Paul Governali, himself a former NFL quarterback, found in his study of NFL players active in 1949 that white-collar sons were no longer a majority on team rosters, and barely outnumbered blue-collar players (46.6 percent to 45.5 percent). The white-collar fathers in this sample were still dominated by high level managers, businessmen and professionals (61.0 percent), but artisans no longer predominated in blue-collar ranks. More fathers were unskilled workers (42.5 percent) than skilled workers (40.0 percent). Upward mobility was also reflected in the ethnic origins of this sample. One-third of all the players were second-generation immigrants, including one-fourth of either eastern European (15 percent) or Italian (9 percent) extraction.[33]

In the 1950s when most American workers were white-collar, the majority of football players were blue-collar in origin (52.2 percent); two out of five (40.5 percent) were white-collar (see table 2). Just one-third of the manual fathers were artisans, and the rest were mainly semiskilled factory operatives. Yet even in this period of working-class dominance, sons of miners still made up just a handful of the sample (5.4 percent). Despite their social origins, these athletes were still very well educated. Virtually all pros active in the 1950s were college men, and among the respondents to a questionnaire, a remarkable 89.3 percent had a college degree, including 29.5 percent with advanced degrees. Players in this era of low salaries were farsighted men with long-term aspirations that extended well beyond their active gridiron careers.[34]

NFL players active in the 1950s married well despite their somewhat modest origins. About seventy percent of their spouses had attended college, and half earned a degree. Three-fifths of the wives (63.2 percent) had white-collar backgrounds, and one-third (32.1 percent) had blue-collar origins. Consequently one-third (32.8 percent) of the players married up—double the rate who married down (14.7 percent). Athletes from relatively humble backgrounds met and romanced girls they would never have met had they not gone to college.[35]

The social background of men active in the 1950s is very similar to that of long-term journeymen players active in the 1970s, and almost identical to that of star players active from the 1950s to the early 1980s (see table 2). In the 1970s, for instance, nearly two-fifths (37.1 percent) of star players were white-collar in origin, well over half (57.2 percent) were blue-collar, and the rest (5.7 percent) were sons of farmers. A marked distinction existed in the class origins of white and black stars. The top white players were almost evenly distributed by nonmanual (44.4 percent) and manual (48.8 percent) origins, but black stars were overwhelmingly from blue-collar households (64.7 percent); just three out of ten (29.4 percent) were from white-collar backgrounds. Further-

Table 3

Occupational Status of Retired Professional Football Players
Active in the 1930s and 1950s

Occupational Category	1930s n = 48 (%)	1950s n = 114 (%)
High white-collar		
Professionals	16.7	15.8
Managers, high officials, and		
major proprietors	35.4	29.8
Subtotal	52.1	45.6
Low white-collar		
Clerks, sales, and kindred workers	18.75	21.9
Semiprofessionals	6.25	15.8
Petty proprietors, managers, and		
low officials	18.75	15.8
Subtotal	43.75	53.5
Total white-collar	95.8	99.1
Blue-collar	2.1	0
Farm	2.1	0.9
Grand total	100.0	100.0

Source: Study data collected by Riess.
$p < .001$.

more, black manual breadwinners were usually unskilled or semi-skilled and the few black nonmanual parents held low level white-collar positions.[36]

The average tenure of NFL players since the 1930s has been about three and a half years, leaving them, like other athletes, in need of subsequent lifelong employment. Professional football players active between the 1930s and 1950s have been extremely successful after their playing days ended (see table 3). About ninety-eight percent ended up in white-collar jobs, often high level and well-paying. Slightly more than half (52.1 percent) of the 1930s group became executives, major proprietors, or professionals, an impressive accomplishment, especially for men who entered the labor force during the depression. The 1950s players were slightly less likely to secure high white-collar jobs (45.6 percent), and the majority ended up in low white-collar occupations (53.5 percent), mainly in sales, which provided an opportunity to take advantage of their fame. Overall, men from the 1950s were twice as likely to end up as salesmen or sales managers (22.8 percent) as men from the 1930s (12.5 percent), and almost twice as likely to become football coaches, including teacher/coaches (14.9 percent to 8.3 percent). The differential opportunities in coaching were mainly due to the growing number of jobs in the NFL.[37]

Players active in the 1960s and 1970s have continued to be very successful in securing white-collar employment, although the proportion in highly prestigious posts has declined. A survey of the subsequent careers of the 1963 champion Chicago Bears reported that they all had white-collar jobs. Two-fifths (38.5 percent) had high level careers, including corporate vice-presidents, a professor, and an engineer. Nearly one-fourth (23.1 percent) of the rest had sports related jobs. A study of NFL alumni active in the 1970s who averaged over eleven years in the league found that about ninety-five percent had secured nonmanual jobs, and nearly all (97.7 percent) were earning at least twenty thousand dollars a year. Since retirement, about half (48 percent) had held sales positions and/or were entrepreneurs (45 percent), jobs where athletic fame could be of assistance. They were also commonly employed in middle management (32 percent), or coaching and scouting (23 percent). The slight change in retirement patterns from the earlier cohorts reflected the growing opportunities to remain active in the sport after retirement from playing, as well as the lower educational attainments of football players active in the 1970s; fifty-seven percent of this sample had college degrees.[38]

The well-paid players of the 1980s differ from prior groups of pro football players by race and level of education. In 1982 fifty-five percent of players were black and 31.5 percent had college degrees. Graduation rates correlated with race. In 1982 just one-fifth of blacks (20.1 percent), but two-fifths of whites (38.2 percent) were graduates. Their poor academic records are the product of inadequate scholastic preparation, the enormous time committed to football during the academic year (which made it hard to take the necessary course loads), and the lack of interest or aptitude in academics among many Division I football players who had enrolled in college to study football and prepare for a lucrative NFL career. NFL players in the 1980s were treated royally and well compensated for a couple of years, and only thereafter did reality set in. Studies of men who retired in the early 1980s found that about ten percent could not secure a white-collar job after leaving the gridiron. While less of a decline than that suffered by boxers or baseball players, it is substantial in comparison to the careers of prior groups of NFL players. We are already seeing stories published about former Superbowl players who have become destitute and homeless.[39]

More professional team athletes make their living playing in the NFL than in any other sport. In 1988, for instance, there were 1,316 places on pro football rosters. However, average players have only recently made a lot of money, and usually just for a few years. Back in the 1930s players were predominantly middle-class sons who used the sport to make a decent living and get a head start on a lifelong career. In the 1950s the athletes were mainly upwardly mobile young men, but, as in the case of earlier players, their long-term success was more a product of their good education than of the fame earned in the NFL. If football played a role in the future prosperity of 1950s players, it was mainly because they had used it to secure a college scholarship to pay for their education. This career pattern seems to have changed once NFL players began to be paid huge salaries. They saw no need to defer gratification and they were no longer graduating from college. How well today's players will cope with their financial situation once the cheering stops remains to be seen.

PROFESSIONAL BASEBALL

Baseball is the oldest professionalized team sport in America. Beginning in 1860 with James Creighton of the Brooklyn Excelsiors, players were compensated for their playing time, either in cash or with an easy job or government sinecure. The Cincinnati Red Stockings in 1869 were the first team openly to pay all players, whose salaries ranged from $600 to $2,000 for the season. Two years later the National Association of Base Ball Players was organized, and during the league's five-year existence salaries averaged from $1,300 to $1,600, considerably more than skilled workers then earned. In 1876 the National Association was supplanted by the National League of Professional Baseball Clubs, which tried to keep wages in line by the introduction of a reserve clause in 1879 and a salary cap of $2,000 six years later. The agreement was not completely adhered to and stars like Charles Comiskey earned as much as $6,000 a year in the late 1880s. However, a new $2,400 limit was established in 1891 after the demise of the rival Players' League and the merger of the National League and the American Association, organized back in 1882. Players in the 1890s averaged under $2,000 a year, and some made as little as $600.[40]

The substantially increased prestige and popularity of baseball after the turn of the century led to the rise of the American League in 1900. It became a major league one year later and instigated a bidding war for top players. By 1910 the average player made about $3,000 a year. Improved salaries and higher status for the occupation encouraged many college athletes to become professional baseball players. Wages continued to rise over the next two decades, reaching an average of about $5,000 by 1923 and $7,500 in 1929. The coming of the depression pushed back salaries in 1936 to about $4,500, which was still outstanding by any yardstick. A $5,000 salary minimum was set after World War II, but the keen competition for jobs in the big leagues kept wages low: salaries in 1950 averaged $12,000 and rose to only $16,000 in 1963. However, in the late 1960s, the players' union, the Major League Players' Association, became very effective under the leadership of Marvin J. Miller, organizing a strike in 1972, and gaining salary arbitration a year later. In 1975 free agency was recognized by the courts in the Messersmith-McNally case. As a result salaries rose to an average of $60,000 in 1975 and $135,000 in 1980. The average salary in 1988 was $413,000.[41]

The first professional baseball players, contrary to conventional wisdom, were urbanites. At a time when about a quarter of the national population was urban, four-fifths of the players in the National Association were city-born. They were mainly from the northeastern cities where the sport had first developed, which undoubtedly gave them a head start. The professional pioneers were drawn from among the best early amateurs, who by occupation during the Civil War had been mainly white-collar (57.1 percent) in metropolitan New York, but blue-collar afterwards (60.7 percent). Historian Melvin L. Adelman found in his masterful study of mid-nineteenth century New York sport that 61.8 percent of the New Yorkers and Brooklynites who played in the National Association were craftsmen and the rest were white-collar workers. Although it paid well, baseball as a new occupation lacked prestige and security; nonmanual workers were less likely to give up a position that offered hopes of future advancement for the risky career of a professional athlete.[42]

A survey of star players born between 1860 and 1879 produced somewhat similar results (see table 4). Over half of these men (53.3 percent) were from blue-collar backgrounds; three out of ten (30 percent) were white-collar; and one-sixth (16.7 percent) were sons of farmers. The rural representation shows the expansion of baseball beyond the urban northeast. While making the majors provided a small number of talented athletes with brief economic mobility, their occupation was not well respected, and retirees had a hard time securing white-collar jobs after baseball. They were generally not well educated, had saved little money, and had no marketable skills. Consequently over one-third of the early professionals active between 1871 and 1882 ended up with blue-collar jobs, an unusually sharp intra-generational decline (see table 6). Half of the retirees ended up in low level nonmanual jobs. There were a few who attained wealth, like sporting goods tycoon Albert G. Spalding, but many of the ex-ballplayers turned small businessmen (12.5 percent) were in enterprises such as saloons, billiards, and bookmaking, which catered to the sporting fraternity and had little social cachet. Nearly one-tenth of the retirees managed taverns or were employed as bartenders.[43]

The social backgrounds of major leaguers changed significantly after the turn of the century as wages rose and the prestige of the occupation improved. A quarter (25.8 percent) of the players active between 1900 and 1919 had attended college, compared to a national average of under five percent of college age men in 1910. Over two-fifths of the players (44.6 percent) had white-collar fathers, more than double the national proportion of white-collar workers in 1910, while just one-third of the players had blue-collar fathers (34.4 percent) and one-fifth had farming fathers (see table 5). Particularly significant was the near total absence of players from the poorest occupations: just 3.3 percent of the major leaguers had unskilled fathers. If we examine star players born between 1880 and 1899, the blue-collar representation is even lower. Just one-fourth of the fathers of these men were blue-collar, and the rest were evenly divided between white-collar and farming jobs. Ballplayers by place of birth were far less urban than in the past (58.4 percent), but urbanites were still overrepresented compared to the national population (45.8 percent in 1910). The decline was a result of the nationalization of baseball, which had expanded well

Table 4

Occupations of Fathers of Major League Baseball Players by Players' Year of Birth

Occupational Category	1840–59 n = 15 (%)	1860–79 n = 30 (%)	1880–99 n = 52 (%)	1900–19 n = 54 (%)	1920–39 n = 48 (%)	1940– n = 38 (%)
White-collar	46.7	30.0	38.5	31.5	27.1	57.9
Blue-collar	40.0	53.3	25.0	44.4	62.5	36.8
Farmer	13.3	26.7	36.5	24.1	10.4	5.3
Grand total	100.0	100.0	100.0	100.0	100.0 ***	100.0 ***

Source: Computed from raw data in David L. Porter, ed., *Biographical Dictionary of American Sports*, vol. 1, *Baseball* (Westport, Conn.: Greenwood Press, 1987).
***p < .001

Table 5

Occupations of Fathers of Major League Baseball Players Active 1900–1958

Occupational Category	1900–19 (%) n = 117	1920–40 (%) n = 100	1941–50 (%) n = 90	1951–58 (%) n = 80	(1941–58) (%) n = 170
White-collar	44.6	48.0	35.5	46.25	40.6
Blue-collar	34.4	30.0	38.9	38.75	38.8
Farmer	20.9	22.0	25.6	15.00	20.6
Grand total	99.9[a] **	100.0 **	100.0	100.0 ***	100.0 ***

Source: Steven A. Riess, *Touching Base: Professional Baseball and American Culture in the Progressive Era* (Westport, Conn.: Greenwood Press, 1980), 172; and computed from unpublished questionnaire data collected by Rudolph Haerle, Jr., and used with permission.
[a] Error due to rounding
**p < .01
***p < .001

beyond its northeastern roots, and the loss of traditional playing areas in older cities caused by rapid urbanization.[44]

The ethnic origins of players active in the first two decades of the century were largely limited to native-born Americans or descendents of Irish and German immigrants. Baseball was very popular among the Irish, who attended games in great numbers and sat in sections like Burkeville at New York's Polo Grounds. One contemporary expert estimated that in the 1890s about one-third of major leaguers were Irish, and they provided a role model for Irish youth who were given positive encouragement to play baseball. We cannot gauge how many players were second- or third-generation Irishmen or Germans seeking an alternate route to success, but it is likely that ethnic major leaguers came from zones of emergence or the suburban fringe (to which early immigrant groups had progressed) rather than from the inner city slums that were the breeding grounds of indigent youth who became boxers and basketball players. Very few baseball players were drawn from the new immigrant groups living in urban squalor. Between 1901 and 1906 there were just five Bohemian, two Jewish, and no Italian rookies; none from any of these groups in 1910; and just one Bohemian and two Italians in 1920 out of 133 first-year men. Inner city youth lacked not only the time and access to playing fields to develop sufficient ballplaying skills, but also parental approval for a strange American game played by grown men running around in short pants.[45]

In the 1920s and 1930s blue-collar youth were again underrepresented on big league rosters (see table 5). Nearly half (48 percent) had nonmanual fathers; just three out of ten (30 percent) had manual fathers; and one-fifth (22 percent) had farming fathers. These players were slightly less urban than the prior cohort (53.7 percent), about equal to the national urban population. During this period the players were still overwhelmingly native-born American or old immigrant stock. In 1929, for example, the five major league teams located in Chicago and New York had a combined total of four regulars of new immigrant descent. As late as 1935 there were just four Italians and two Slavs on the combined rosters of the Dodgers, Giants, and Cubs.[46]

The recruitment pattern changed dramatically in the 1940s with a major decline in the proportion of white-collar players, a big increase in the representation of new immigrants, and the readmittance of blacks to the big leagues. In the 1940s barely one-third of the major leaguers were middle-class in origin (35.5 percent), a 26 percent decline from the period 1920–39 (see table 5). At the same time the blue-collar representation increased from 30 to 38.9 percent. Furthermore, the overwhelming majority of a sample of star players born between 1920 and 1939 were blue-collar. The presence of a blue-collar plurality on big league rosters in the 1940s was tied to a new wave of second- and third-generation southern and eastern Europeans into the majors that began in the late 1930s. By 1941 about 8 percent of big leaguers were Italian and 9.3 percent were Slavic, more than double their share

Table 6
Subsequent Jobs of Retired Major League Baseball Players,
1871–1959

Occupational Category	1871–82 n = 219 (%)	1900–19 n = 478 (%)	1920–39 n = 321 (%)	1940–59 n = 216 (%)	1950–59 n = 790 (%)
High white-collar					
Professionals	1.8	5.9	10.3	7.4	7.8
Managers, high officials, and major proprietors	12.8	19.0	10.0	8.8	14.1
Subtotal	14.6	24.9	20.3	16.2	21.9
Low white-collar					
Clerks, sales, and kindred workers	18.3	10.0	20.2	28.2	24.5
Semiprofessionals	13.2	33.5	24.3	26.9	29.9
Petty proprietors, managers, and low officials	16.9	14.0	12.1	11.6	10.9
Subtotal	48.4	57.5	56.7[a]	66.7	65.3
Total white-collar	63.0	82.4	76.9	82.9	87.3[a]
Farmers	1.4	3.6	4.5	1.9	0.9
Blue-collar					
Skilled	11.9	3.8	4.7	7.4	4.7
Semiskilled and service	21.0	8.8	13.1	6.9	6.5
Unskilled	2.7	1.5	0.9	0.9	0.6
Total blue-collar	35.6	14.1	18.6[a]	15.2	11.8
Grand total	100.0	100.0	100.0	100.0	100.0

Source: Adapted from Steven A. Riess, *Touching Base: Professional Baseball and American Culture in the Progressive Era* (Westport, Conn.: Greenwood Press, 1980), 159, 201; study data of 354 men active between 1920 and 1939 and 243 men active between 1940 and 1959 who played in Chicago or New York; data computed from Rich Marazzi and Len Fiorito, *Aaron to Zuverink: A Nostalgic Look at the Baseball Players of the Fifties* (Briarcliff, N.J.: Stein and Day, 1982).
[a] Error due to rounding

of the national white population. This success reflected the accultura-tion of the sons of the new immigrants who were staying longer in school, playing sports on high school teams, and emulating role models like Al Simmons (Aloysius Szymanski) and Joe DiMaggio; and it also reflected the greater acceptance of the sport among immigrant parents.[47]

Since the 1950s the proportion of players coming from nonmanual families seems to have overtaken that of those from manual back-grounds (see table 5). While the proportion of blue-collar players (38.75 percent) remained about the same, the white-collar players increased by one-third to 46.25 percent compared to the prior decade. This appreciation came at the expense of players with farming fathers, who dropped by two-fifths. The trend in favor of the white-collar player continued in the mid-1960s. Sociologist Harold Charnofsky found that in a sample of seventy-two major leaguers nearly two-thirds (63.3 percent) were white-collar and one-third (36.7 percent) were blue-collar.[48] These results are corroborated by a small sample of star players who were born after 1940 (see table 4): nearly three-fifths (57.9 percent) were white-collar; one third (36.9 percent) blue-collar; and the rest (5.3 percent) farmers. The social origin of these athletes was strongly tied to race. As in other sports, black professional athletes were usually drawn from lower socioeconomic circumstances than their white peers. Among the star players born since 1940, three-fourths of the white players (76.9 percent) had nonmanual fathers while four-fifths of the blacks (83.3 percent) came from blue-collar families.[49]

The modern day baseball player has been much more successful in his second career by comparison to the major leaguer of the late nineteenth century, but less successful than either former basketball or football players (see table 6). After the average three- to four-year major league career, and a few more years down in the minors, ballplayers retired at relatively early ages when most men were just getting established in their careers. The new jobs seldom paid as well as baseball, but retirees fared better than was popularly believed. Four-fifths of the players active from 1900 to 1919 had white-collar employment after baseball and similar results were achieved by players active in the periods 1920–39 (76.9 percent) and 1940–59 (82.9 percent). Future farmers were always a small proportion, never more than 4.5 percent. This is surprising since so many players came from rural backgrounds, but understandable because the experiences and possible fame derived from playing professional sports were of no benefit to ranchers or dairy farmers. The least successful retirees ended up with manual jobs, ranging from 11.8 percent of players active in the 1950s to nearly one-fifth (18.6 percent) of their predecessors active in the period 1920–39.[50]

Unlike the pro football players who often ended up in high level managerial and professional jobs, most retired baseball players became low level white-collar workers. In all the periods examined, the low white-collar retirees outnumbered the high white-collar players by about three to one. Their familiarity with the game made them very successful in securing baseball-related occupations; the enormous popularity of the sport meant there was wider demand for coaches, managers, and front office personnel. The primary subsequent job of 29.2 percent of the players active in the period 1900–19 was in sports, compared to just 11 percent of men active in 1871–82 when the appeal of the sport was still quite limited. Among players active in the 1950s, one-fourth (24.6 percent) worked primarily in athletics after retirement. Outside of sports the other popular occupations were those that required a lot of direct contact with clients, such as sales, real estate, and insurance. However, fewer players became restaurateurs or saloonkeepers than might have been expected.[51]

While fame may have helped many players in their post-baseball careers, it obviously did not help everyone since there was still a very substantial skidding rate down into the manual job categories, at least until the 1950s. Blue-collar players mainly ended up in semiskilled and service jobs. As Roger Kahn pointed out in *The Boys of Summer*, even players from the great Brooklyn Dodgers teams of the 1950s could end up working in construction, like Carl Furillo, or indigent, like Sandy Amoros.[52]

The future success of an ex-major leaguer depended on a variety of factors including his fame, tenure in the majors, social background, and education. Fame was an important factor in helping an individual get a sports-related job and, more importantly, his first position after baseball. In the long run more important than fame were the player's first job, and especially his education and family background. For example, in the period 1900–19, over ninety-three percent of college-educated players secured white-collar jobs and the rest were mainly farmers. By comparison, two-thirds (67.5 percent) of the non-college men secured white-collar jobs and a quarter ended up in blue-collar jobs. Social background was nearly as important. The overwhelming majority of players from this era whose fathers were white-collar (85 percent) also ended up white-collar. The results were slightly lower for sons of farmers (77 percent), but much lower for sons of manual workers (58 percent). Compared to white-collar sons, a blue-collar son was three times as likely to end up in the blue-collar ranks.[53]

Why was social background so important? Middle-class sons were much more likely to get a good education that prepared them for higher paying and more prestigious jobs. They were encouraged to have high expectations and were taught traditional bourgeois values like thrift, hard work, and deferral of immediate gratification. Players coming from poor families did not receive the same education, encouragement, socialization, and values. They were unprepared for the good wages paid to ballplayers; they frequently indulged in conspicuous consumption, showing off to their friends, their colleagues, and themselves. They were completely unprepared for retirement from the diamond, and often ended up about where they had started out.[54]

CONCLUSION

The notion that professional sport has been an important alternate avenue of social mobility for athletically gifted young men is a powerful concept that has shaped the attitudes and behavior of thousands of young Americans. This inspiring myth was a gross exaggeration, but there were always enough rags to riches stories to convince people of its veracity. Sport has certainly been as democratic in its recruitment policies as any other high paying, legitimate occupation. Poverty, a lack of education, and the absence of good connections did not disqualify anyone from becoming a prize fighter or major league baseball player. Impoverishment could be overcome by basketball or football players: even after college became necessary for recruits, they could earn a scholarship and begin their climb towards a professional career. Once at the top level of sport, an athlete earned considerably more money over a brief period of time than he could have at any other job; a handful would even become rich. Since the mid-1970s, participation in team sports has become extremely lucrative, and average basketball, baseball, and football players earn several hundred thousand dollars a year.

Yet the reality is that professional athletics has not been a major source of vertical mobility for lower-class youth. The value of professional sport as a means of advancement has depended upon the ability of disadvantaged young men to enter the field of sport, achieve success in that arena, and then continue to fare well after retirement from athletics. Poor white ethnics had no barriers preventing them from breaking into boxing or basketball, but it took a long time before eastern and southern Europeans became successful in baseball or football. Blacks had even less access because all professional team sports prohibited their participation for certain periods of time, and even boxing was blighted by bigotry. Since the integration of professional team sports in the late 1940s, blacks have gained more intergenerational mobility than any other ethnic group. Blacks not only dominate prize fighting, basketball and football, but they are the most likely to have come from lower-class origins and thus benefited the most from their athletic opportunities.

The recruitment patterns of the leading professional sports have varied markedly by social class. Only boxing has always drawn its participants exclusively from the lowest socioeconomic groups. The original recruitment pattern for basketball players was quite similar to that for prize fighters, but as the sport gained in popularity, the socioeconomic backgrounds of basketball participants became more heterogeneous. Thus at least a small proportion of NBA players were in the 1950s and 1960s middle-class sons. There were even a few, like Bill Bradley, of higher social rank.

The recruitment matrix for baseball and football was more complicated. The first professional baseball and football players were mainly from blue-collar artisan backgrounds. Once these sports became more remunerative and more prestigious, middle-class players began to predominate. Consequently, fewer jobs went to upwardly mobile lower-class sons. The pattern changed again, in the 1940s for baseball and a decade later for football, since blue-collar players again outnumbered their white-collar colleagues. In the 1960s the social composition of baseball players changed again in favor of athletes from nonmanual backgrounds, while blue-collar football players have continued to outnumber their white-collar peers. Overall neither baseball nor football has drawn a significant proportion of recruits from the bottom of the social ladder, although both sports have been open to working-class folk.

The small number of professional sportsmen who made it to the top could not rely upon their athletic careers to sustain whatever intergenerational mobility they had achieved, because their tenure was very short and they seldom saved enough to set them up for life upon retirement. Boxers were notorious for falling back into the circumstances from which they had come, and it was also very common for working-class baseball players to skid back into blue-collar employment. A major leaguer's fame helped him secure his first job after baseball, but success in the long run depended more upon his social origins and education than his batting average or earned run average. On the other hand, former pro basketball and football players fared much better, regardless of social origins, because they were so well éducated. Consequently, professional basketball players enjoyed the greatest social mobility, having started out mainly from very humble origins, and almost always (at least until recently) ending up with white-collar jobs. It is too early to predict what will happen to the highly paid athletes of the 1980s, who seldom graduated from college. One would hope that anyone making $520,000 a year (the average NBA salary in 1988) would have the best financial advisors to help him prepare for the future, but only time will tell.

Aspiring athletes tend not to look at the odds of making it to the top or at what happens afterwards, but only at their heroes, like Julius Irving, who did live the rags to riches myth. In an era of million-dollar salaries, certain young men do leap from the ghetto to the penthouse. In reality, however, the investment in time and effort is so great, and the chances of success so remote, that almost all of the hardworking athletes are misappropriating their energies. The concept of sport as a vehicle of social mobility is largely a cultural fiction unless young athletes are using sport as the instrument to secure college entrance and complete an education. The great tragedy of the past two decades is that few elite athletes, be it for lack of preparation, ability, or interest, are benefiting from their free college education—which is the best means for long-term vertical mobility that American sport offers the athletically gifted individual.

NOTES

1. On American social mobility, see the seminal works of Stephen Thernstrom, esp. *Poverty and Progress: Social Mobility in a Nineteenth Century City* (Cambridge: Harvard University Press, 1964) and *The Other Bostonians: Poverty and Progress in the American Metropolis, 1880–1970* (Cambridge: Harvard University Press, 1973). See also Howard P. Chudacoff, *Mobile Americans: Residential and Social Mobility in Omaha, 1880–1920* (New York: Oxford University Press, 1972); Thomas Kessner, *The Golden Door: Italian and Jewish Immigrant Mobility in New York City, 1880–1915* (New York: Oxford University Press, 1977); Clyde and Sally Griffen, *Natives and Newcomers: The Ordering of Opportunity in Mid-Nineteenth Century Poughkeepsie* (Cambridge:

Harvard University Press, 1989); Olivier Zunz, *The Changing Face of Inequality: Urbanization, Industrial Development, and Immigrants in Detroit, 1880–1980* (Chicago: University of Chicago Press, 1982); and John Bodnar, Roger Simon, and Michael Weber, *Lives of Their Own: Blacks, Italians, and Poles in Pittsburgh* (Urbana, Ill.: University of Illinois Press, 1982).

2. Motion pictures, the daily press, and literature have been important vehicles for promoting the myths of sport. Among the movies that support a mythic view are *Golden Boy* (1937), *Pride of the Yankees* (1942), *Body and Soul* (1947), *The Jackie Robinson Story* (1950), *Somebody Up There Likes Me* (1956), and more recently, *The Natural* (1984) and *Hoosiers* (1987). See Ronald Bergan, *Sports in the Movies* (New York: Proteus Books, 1982). For the early influence of sports journalism, see Christian K. Messenger, *Sport and the Spirit of Play in American Fiction: Hawthorne to Faulkner* (New York: Columbia University Press, 1981), 95–100. Juvenile sports literature is full of false images of the reality of sport, but adult readers of works like Ring Lardner's *You Know Me Al: A Busher's Story* (New York: Charles Scribner's Sons, 1914) and "Alibi Ike" (1915) in *Ring Lardner's Best Stories*; (Garden City, N.Y.: Garden City, 1938) also receive inaccurate images of the national pastime. On sport literature and mythology see Messenger, *Sport and the Spirit of Play*, esp. chaps. 5–9; and Michael Oriard, *Dreaming of Heroes: American Sports Fiction, 1868–1980* (Chicago: Nelson-Hall, 1962), chaps. 2, 4, 6. For scholars identifying sport as an alternate avenue of social mobility, see Leonard Dinnerstein and David M. Reimers, *Ethnic Americans: A History of Immigration and Assimilation* (New York: Dodd, Mead, 1975), 136–37; and Neil D. Isaacs, *Jock Culture USA* (New York: Norton, 1978), 168.

3. *New York Times*, Feb. 6, Feb. 27, May 1, Oct. 2, 1977; Howard L. Nixon, *Sport and the American Dream* (New York: Leisure Press, 1984), 160–64, 179–83; Wilbert M. Leonard II and Jonathan E. Reyman, "The Odds of Attaining Professional Athletic Status: Refining the Computations," *Sociology of Sport Journal* 5 (June, 1988): 162–69. For summaries of the sociological literature on sport and mobility, see Rudolph K. Haerle, Jr., "Education, Athletic Scholarships, and the Occupational Career of the Professional Athlete," *Sociology of Work and Occupations* 2 (1975): 373–403; Emil Bend and B. M. Petrie, "Sport Participation, Scholastic Success and Social Mobility," *Exercise and Sports Sciences Reviews* 5 (1977): 1–44; Jomills Henry Braddock II, "Race, Sports and Social Mobility: A Critical Review," *Sociological Symposium* 30 (Spring, 1980): 13–38; Steven A. Riess, "Sport and the American Dream: A Review Essay," *Journal of Social History* 14 (Fall, 1980): 295–303.

4. Valuable historiographic essays on sport history include Melvin L. Adelman, "Academicians and Athletics: Historians' View of American Sport," *Maryland Historian* 4 (May, 1973): 123–37; idem, "Academicians and American Athletics: A Decade of Progress," *Journal of Sport History* 10 (Spring, 1983): 80–106; and Stephen Hardy, "The City and the Rise of American Sport, 1820–1920," *Exercise and Sports Sciences Reviews* 9 (1983): 183–219. For a survey of the historical literature on sport and mobility, see Riess, "Sport and the American Dream," 295–303.

5. Melvin L. Adelman, *A Sporting Time: New York City and the Rise of Modern Athletics, 1820–70* (Urbana: University of Illinois Press, 1986), 235–37.

6. Adelman, *Sporting Time*, 237; Gustavus Myers, *History of Tammany Hall* (New York, 1901), 189; Alfred H. Lewis, *Richard Croker* (New York: Life, 1901), 43–44; Elliott J. Gorn, "'Good-Bye Boys, I Die a True American': Homicide, Nativism, and Working-Class Culture in Antebellum New York City," *Journal of American History* 74

(Sept., 1987): 387–410. The best study of early American boxing is Elliott J. Gorn, *The Manly Art: Bare-Knuckle Prize Fighting in America* (Ithaca: Cornell University Press, 1986).

7. Michael Isenberg, *John L. Sullivan and His America* (Urbana: University of Illinois Press, 1988), 387–88; Benjamin G. Rader, *American Sports: From the Age of Folk Games to the Age of Spectators* (Englewood Cliffs, N.J.: Prentice-Hall, 1983), 99; Gorn, *Manly Art*, chap. 7.

8. Steven A. Riess, *City Games: The Evolution of American Urban Society and the Rise of Sports* (Urbana: University of Illinois Press, 1989), 106–13, 115–16.

9. Thomas J. Jenkins, "Changes in Ethnic Succession and Racial Representation among Professional Boxers: A Study in Ethnic Succession" (M.A. thesis, University of Chicago, 1955), 15, 21; Riess, *City Games*, 109–10.

10. Ibid. Also see Steven A. Riess, "A Fighting Chance: The Jewish-American Boxing Experience, 1890–1940," *American Jewish History* 74 (Mar., 1988): 223–54.

11. Riess, *City Games*, 115–16. On mixed bouts in New York City, see *New York Times*, Dec. 29, 1911, Jan. 7, 1912, June 6, 1915, Jan. 17, Feb. 18, 1916; *New York World*, Jan. 17, June 29, Aug. 8, 1916; "Smith-Langford Cancelled," *Boxing and Sporting World*, Oct. 4, 1913, p. 4.

12. A. O. Edmonds, *Joe Louis* (Grand Rapids: Wm. Eerdmann, 1972), chap. 7; Lawrence W. Levine, *Black Culture and Black Consciousness: Afro-American Folk Thought from Slavery to Freedom* (New York: Oxford University Press, 1977), 433–38. For an excellent discussion of black boxing, see Jeffrey T. Sammons, *Beyond the Ring: The Role of Boxing in American Society* (Urbana: University of Illinois Press, 1988).

13. S. Kirson Weinberg and Henry Arond, "The Occupational Culture of the Boxer," *American Journal of Sociology* 57 (Mar., 1952): 460–61; Nathan Hare, "A Study of the Black Fighter," *Black Scholar* 3 (Nov., 1971): 2–8.

14. Randy Roberts, *Papa Jack: Jack Johnson and the Era of White Hopes* (New York: Macmillan, 1983), 90; U.S. Cong., Senate, Judiciary Committee, *Professional Boxing Hearings before Subcommittee on Antitrust and Monopoly*, 86th Cong., 2d sess., Pursuant to S. Res. 238, Dec. 5–15, 1960 (Washington, D.C.: GPO, 1961), 655–66; Barney Ross and Martin Abrahamson, *No Man Stands Alone: The True Story of Barney Ross* (Philadelphia: Lippincott, 1957), 141, 159; Weinberg and Arond, "Occupational Culture of the Boxer," 460.

15. Jack Lawrence, "The Antiques of Fistiana," *Ring*, June, 1930, pp. 31–32; Hare, "Study of the Black Fighter," 6–8.

16. Riess, *City Games*, 112; Riess, "A Fighting Chance," 253 n.65.

17. Weinberg and Arond, "The Occupational Culture of the Boxer," 469; Hare, "Study of the Black Fighter," 6–8.

18. Larry Fox, *Illustrated History of Basketball* (New York: Hawthorne Books, 1974), 9–46; Ted Vincent, *Mudville's Revenge: The Rise and Fall of American Sport* (New York: Seaview, 1981), 226–52.

19. Fox, *Basketball*, 46–47; Vincent, *Mudville's Revenge*, 247–56, 279–81, 290–91.

20. Glenn Dickey, *The History of Professional Basketball since 1896* (New York: Stein and Day, 1982), 25–31, 37–42; Fox, *Basketball*, 57; Vincent, *Mudville's Revenge*, 281–82, 289–305; Rader, *American Sports*, 351; Brenton Welling, Jonathan Tasini, and Don Cook, "Basketball: Business is Booming," *Business Week*, Mar. 4, 1985, pp. 75–76.

21. Computed from biographical data in Ronald L. Mendell, *Who's Who in Basketball* (New Rochelle, N.Y.: Arlington House, 1973). Data on college education was drawn

from William Clyde DeVane, *Higher Education in Twentieth-Century America* (Cambridge: Harvard University Press, 1965), 59.

22. Joseph Durso, *The Sports Factory* (New York: Quadrangle, 1975), 81. Percentages computed from biographical data in Mendell, *Who's Who in Basketball.*

23. Computed from biographical data in Mendell, *Who's Who in Basketball.* On the geographic origins of All-Americans, see *Chicago Sun-Times*, Dec. 12, 1983. For a discussion of the geographic origins of Division I basketball players, see John F. Rooney, Jr., *A Geography of American Sport: From Cabin Creek to Anaheim* (Reading, Mass.: Addison-Wesley, 1974), esp. chaps. 7, 10.

24. By comparison, in 1982 baseball was 19 percent black and football 55 percent black. On inner city basketball, see Pete Axthelm, *The City Game: Basketball in New York from the World Champion Knicks to the World of the Playgrounds* (New York: Harper's Magazine Press, 1970); Rick Telander, *Heaven is a Playground* (New York: St. Martin's Press, 1976). Basketball was (and is) a central element of growing up in New York's ghettoes; it kept kids busy, away from gangs, and gave them self-esteem and high hopes. Black inner-city ball stresses an individualistic style of play (very different from the emphasis on teamwork of earlier ghetto youth) that lacked the precision of small town basketball. Players faked out opponents, blocked shots, and stuffed the basketball. For insightful comments explaining black superiority in professional sports as a consequence of limited alternative recreational opportunities for inner-city youth, see Bob Gibson with Phil Pepe, *From Ghetto to Glory: The Story of Bob Gibson* (Englewood Cliffs, N.J.: Prentice-Hall, 1968), 6.

25. Rader, *American Sports*, 353; Durso, *Sports Factory*, 76. The current graduation rate among Division I basketball players is 27 percent. Richard Lapchick interview, "Nightline," ABC Network, Jan. 24, 1989.

26. On the early days of professional football, see J. Thomas Jable, "The Birth of Professional Football: Pittsburgh Athletic Clubs Ring in Professionals in 1892," *Western Pennsylvania Historical Magazine* 62 (Apr., 1979): 136–47; Tom Bennett et al., *The NFL's Official Encyclopedic History of Professional Football* (New York: Macmillan, 1979), 11–16; Emil Klosinski, *Pro Football in the Days of Rockne* (New York: Carleton Press, 1970); Harry A. March, *Professional Football: Its Ups and Downs* (New York: J. B. Lyon, 1934).

27. Robert Curran, *Pro Football's Rag Days* (Englewood Cliffs, N.J.: Prentice-Hall, 1970); Rader, *American Sports*, 182–86.

28. Bennett, *NFL*, 25–27; March, *Pro Football*, 250–51; Curran, *Pro Football's Rag Days*, 107, 121, 140, 184; Rader, *American Sports*, 253.

29. Rader, *American Sports*, 347, 353; *Chicago Tribune*, Dec. 1, 1988.

30. Ethnicity of players was computed from lists of NFL players in David S. Neft, Richard M. Cohen, and Jordan A. Deutsch, *Pro Football: The Early Years, 1895–1959* (Ridgefield, Conn., 1973).

31. College attendance computed from ibid. For comparative data with baseball players, see Steven A. Riess, *Touching Base: Professional Baseball and American Culture in the Progressive Era* (Westport, Conn.: Greenwood Press, 1980), 85. Biographical data on players active in the 1930s and 1950s was drawn from a questionnaire sent in 1984 to 400 randomly selected former NFL players. I received 164 usable responses from retirees (41 percent rate of return). Forty-eight of the respondents had played in the 1930s and the rest (116) in the 1950s. It is not altogether unlikely that respondents were more successful than nonrespondents. However, the results are consistent with impressionistic evidence as corroborated in my discussions with football scholar C. Robert

Barnett, who has done extensive oral history work with former pro football players. See, e.g., C. Robert Barnett and Linda Terhune, "When the Tanks Were Tops," *River Cities Monthly*, Sept., 1979, p. 18. My sampling results are also very similar to a sociological study conducted by Paul Governali, "The Professional Football Player: His Vocational Status" (M.A. thesis, Teachers' College, Columbia University, 1951), 49. I thank Rick Korch and the NFL Alumni Association for their assistance.

32. Computed from study data. For a full discussion, see Steven A. Riess, "A Social Profile of the Professional Football Player: Past and Present," in *American Professional Sports: Social, Historical, Economic and Legal Perspectives*, ed. Paul Staudohar and J. A. Mangan (Urbana: University of Illinois Press, in press).

33. Governali, "Professional Football Player," 52, 53.

34. See note 31 above.

35. Ibid.

36. Ibid. Data on star players was computed from biographical data in David Porter, ed., *Biographical Dictionary of American Sports*, vol. 2, *Football* (Westport, Conn.: Greenwood Press, 1987). Data on journeymen who averaged about eleven years in the NFL was drawn from Larry Van Roe, "A Descriptive Study of the Effects of Career Termination upon Journeyman Professional Football Players" (Ed.D. diss., University of Georgia, 1984), 135.

37. Computed from Neft, Cohen, and Deutsch, *Pro Football* and study data; John Underwood, "Student Athletes: The Sham, the Shame," *Sports Illustrated*, May 19, 1980, p. 60; Jill Lieber, "Pro Football," ibid., Dec. 15, 1986, p. 72; *Los Angeles Times*, Jan. 27, 1986, sec. 3, p. 32, col. 1 (I am indebted to Paul Staudohar for the latter two citations). Football coaches were designated as semiprofessionals with the exception of high school teachers/coaches who were identified in table 3 as professionals. One could make a strong argument that by prestige, income, and responsibility, head football coaches at major universities, and NFL coaches, especially since the 1960s, should be categorized as major executives.

38. Rick Korch, "The Year of the Bear," *NFL Alumni Legends Magazine*, July 29, 1983, 1E–5E (my thanks to Rick Korch for this citation); Van Roe, "Effects of Career Termination," 167, 189.

39. Computed from *The Sporting News Football Register, 1982* (St. Louis: Sporting News, 1982); *Los Angeles Times*, Jan. 27, 1986, sec. 3, p. 32, col. 1; Van Roe, "Effects of Career Termination," 167; Gerard F. Middlemiss, "Occupational Attainment of Former Professional Football Players" (Ed.D. diss., Rutgers University, 1984), 85.

40. On early baseball compensation, see Adelman, *A Sporting Time*, 133–34; Harold Seymour, *Baseball*, vol. 1, *The Early Years* (New York: Oxford University Press, 1960), 47–48, 52, 117–20; David Q. Voigt, *American Baseball*, vol. 1, *From Gentlemen's Game to the Commissioner's System* (Norman: University of Oklahoma Press, 1966), 140–41.

41. Riess, *Touching Base*, 163–64; Paul M. Gregory, *The Baseball Player: An Economic Study* (Washington, D.C.: Public Affairs Press, 1956), 93; U.S. Cong., House Judiciary Committee, *Organized Baseball. Hearings before the Subcommittee on Study of Monopoly Power*, 82nd Cong., 1st sess., 1951, Serial 1, Part 6 (Washington, D.C.: GPO, 1952), 1610–11; David Q. Voigt, *American Baseball*, vol. 3, *From Postwar Expansion to the Electronic Age* (University Park, Penn.: Pennsylvania State University Press, 1983), 57, 58; Rader, *American Sports*, 346–47, 352, 353.

42. Adelman, *A Sporting Time*, 156, 177, 179. While the best players were blue-collar, overall most players before (64.3 percent) and after (69.2 percent) the Civil War

were white-collar. Ibid., 155, 175. Adelman found that just one-fourth (26.0 percent) of his sample of early professional players in the National Association fell into blue-collar jobs after retirement, which indicated a fair measure of long-term social mobility for the early players. Ibid., 179.

43. Data on stars drawn from biographical data in David L. Porter, ed., *Biographical Dictionary of American Sports*, vol. 1, *Baseball* (Westport, Conn.: Greenwood Press, 1987). On the mobility patterns of players active between 1871 and 1882, see Riess, *Touching Base*, 157–60.

44. Riess, *Touching Base*, 171–73, 180–83.

45. Ibid., 184–91.

46. Computed from raw data generously provided by Rudolph K. Haerle, Jr., based on a 1958 questionnaire sent to 876 former major leaguers, of whom 335 (38.2 percent) responded. See Rudolph K. Haerle, Jr., "Career Patterns and Career Contingencies of Professional Baseball Players: An Occupational Analysis," in *Sport and Social Order: Contributions to the Sociology of Sport*, ed. Donald W. Ball and John W. Loy (Reading, Mass.: Addison-Wesley, 1975), 510 n. 4. Geographic origins of players were based on a sample of 354 major leaguers who played in Chicago or New York between 1920 and 1939. Their birthplaces were taken from *The Baseball Encyclopedia* (New York: Macmillan, 1969). On ethnicity, see Riess, *Touching Base*, 191.

47. Computed from raw data in Haerle questionnaire; Riess, *Touching Base*, 191–92.

48. Computed from raw data in Haerle questionnaire; Charnofsky found that the mid 1960s players were from families that had enjoyed considerable intra-generational mobility. When the players were growing up, three-fifths (59.9 percent) were living in blue-collar households; but by the time they were adults, nearly two-thirds of their fathers were white-collar. See Harold Charnofsky, "The Major League Baseball Player: A Sociological Study" (Ph.D. diss. University of Southern California, 1969), 130.

49. Data on star players computed from biographical information in Porter, *Baseball*.

50. Riess, *Touching Base*, 198–206; Voigt, *American Baseball*, 3: 58; and study sample drawn from 243 major leaguers active between 1940 and 1959 who played in Chicago or New York. Occupational data for players active in the period 1920–39 and 1940–59 was collected from The Vertical Files, National Baseball Library, Cooperstown, N.Y.

51. Riess, *Touching Base*, 199–204.

52. Roger Kahn, *The Boys of Summer* (New York: New American Library, 1973), chap. 10.

53. Riess, *Touching Base*, 206–207.

54. Ibid., 207–208.

Modern Criticism of Sport

ON THE BOULEVARD Saint Michel in Paris there are many fine bookstores. Some specialize in literature and some in the visual arts. A sprawling bookstore near the University of Paris purports to be nearly complete regarding the scholarly or at least earnest literature from French presses that deal with history and the behavioral and social sciences. Recently I entered the store and approached a male clerk who seemed predisposed to be amiable.

"Is there a section of this fine establishment that deals with the history or with the social aspects of sport?" I asked.

In the precise, nasal tones employed in a metropolis to deal with a strayed yokel, with irony in his third word, he replied, "No, I regret that we do not deal with sport." And indeed, the French intellectual establishment, for which this splendid undertaking was a commercial outlet, does not and shall not have anything to do with sport, which, though it exists and flourishes in France as everywhere else, is not an accepted part of *civilisation*.

There is sport criticism in France, but it is of the same sort that we find in the American sports pages: carping concerned with performance, movements of money, and the characters of star practitioners and managers—all of whom, it seems, merit and get close scrutiny. There are statistically backed discussions of salaries and budgets and of sports performances that are fine or disappointing. In France some aspects of the criticism are different from American skepticism and carping. Due to the stifling of provincial culture that has been a government policy for almost a thousand years now, French sports journalism, though separated from national intellectual life, is published and read nationwide. And sports writers—largely due to the overarching role of the daily sports newspaper, *L'Equipe*, which demands good language—usually write well.

The French pattern or level of sports criticism is characteristic of that in most of the industrialized world. Sports writing is critical only when it deals with performance. It is chauvinistic, optimistic, and aimed at non-intellectual readers. It occupies the second sections of even the best newpapers in Italy, Spain, and Scandinavia.

In the Socialist world—not only the not-yet-disintegrated Soviet bloc, but also in places like Cuba—sport is inextricably intermixed with state policy and official ideology. In these areas of the world, sport criticism—both shallow commentary and the more profound kind that is analytically ideological and earnest in a social-skeptical way—is almost unimaginable. However, in the Soviet bloc, because of the high status of sports writers and the stultifying official expectations of writers on other sorts of current affairs, the level of sports writing tends to be—stylistically, at least—rather rich. In some Third World countries, there is a sort of fresh wonder, a pleasure in the heroism, theatrical spectacle, and poetic inspiration that lies awaiting happy journalistic exploitation in sport. The modern novelty of sport receives almost as much attention in print as politics, religion, and the arts combined.

Despite the extent of sports literature at this popular level, it has seemed to a few of us that sport is a subject of such financial dimensions, social intricacy, and theatrical potential that it merits much more earnest pondering than it has received. The worldwide triumph and flourishing of modern sport must mean something. Should not the more socially critical of us be posing the question, "What does sport mean?" Should there not be more of us reveling in the excitement of doing careful watching, thinking and talking and also avoiding the ritualistic "manchat" (Robert Lipsyte's fine neologism) of sportstalk and attempting to see where the spectacle fits in?

The story I will tell is not bleak. There are, here and there, fine, profound, and perhaps nascently inspiring sports critics seeking and slowly finding more readers.

As the magisterial French detailer of *"la longue durée"* in history, Fernand Braudel, might say, "But first a little bit of history." We must look at the background of the productively controversy-ridden historiography of sport. There is growing consensus among analytical historians that sport today is fundamentally unlike any sort of public manifestations that preceded its birth and rich flourishing.[1] Sport, broadly observed in all its variety, is closely intertwined with and dependent upon the industrial world's concepts of time and space. The peculiar nature of modern sport has been described in some detail by Allen Guttmann in the first book to appear in English giving the distinguishing characteristics of sport as we know it. Guttmann lists the novelties of our sport as the following: secularism, equality, specialization, rationalization, bureaucracy, quantification, and records.[2] The list of characteristics may vary, the points to stress may be different, but ever more sports scholars within the established areas of social analysis accept that contemporary sport is quite new and cannot be analyzed usefully unless one keeps in mind that our sports act as reinforcers and legitimizers of the modern political status quo.

Guttmann and I agree. But rather than ruthlessly characterizing the state of things now, I have been more interested in determining how things got to be this way. And so I will restate here in a more schematic form matters that I have discussed elsewhere.[3]

It sounds abrupt and simple, but the forms of our sports had their origins in some peculiar and portentous developments in English society in the late eighteenth and early nineteenth centuries. Though these novelties inspired a lot of proud and anecdotal literature in English, the origins of horse racing, the publication of rules for team sports such as cricket and football, the establishment of specific parameters for events, and the formation of ceremonies for intercollegiate athletics were all so natural, so organic, so gracefully welcomed in the various social milieus in which they flourished and spread, that the critics of English (and later American) society were scarcely aware (as most remain) of what was going on.

There is a vast literature on the peculiarity of English society. Much of this literature is old and is based on primary observation by continental visitors as early as the seventeenth century. Travelers saw that lower-class Englishmen were more likely to be landless than their European counterparts, and hence to be working for wages; had more money, were more mobile, and were regular eaters of meat. Subsequent critics suggested that the relative robustness of a wide range of Englishmen may have opened them to a lustier exploitation of the possibilities of play. Other observers, and I think these should be more interesting to us, have noted that the English were innovators in economic activities that required a peculiar view of time: English capitalists viewed time as an investment commodity. They had an attitude

that the Germans who have written on this topic describe by employing a marvelous word: *Langfristigezeitinvestitionsperspektive* (long-
term-time-investment perspective). What we are hovering about here
is the Industrial Revolution and its transformation or rationalization of
production, which we now believe provided the economic foundations
of modern society and modern life.

Where, when, and why did modern life begin? This is a central
problem around which circle most of the truly original historians of our
century. Fernand Braudel (1902–86) is the author of the acclaimed
three-volume *Civilization and Capitalism: 15th to 18th Centuries.*[4] In
this he examines yet again a central problem—that is, how did Western Europe conquer the world? Braudel expands the area that one
must consider as the breeding ground of modern culture. He would
have us believe that, despite mind-sets that were evident in many
places in Europe, it was the English who spread the specific techniques of mass production and money management that were most
easily and effectively imitated—at first and for a long time most spec-
tacularly in the United States. But most of us know this.[5]

That there were contemporary observers and critics of the social
changes accompanying the transformation of the material bases of society goes without saying. And, significantly enough, the most original
and influential critics watched developments in Britain and used their
insights for prophesies of stupendous impact. I am referring to Karl
Marx and Friedrich Engels. On the other hand, almost no one noticed
as English and subsequently, American sports evolved, proliferated,
and were everywhere adapted. The forms and allegiances of sport were
well suited—were charming reinforcers, in fact—for a daily life of de-
racination, schedules, citified crowds, bustle, and literacy. The "fit" or
integration of the new myths of sport into daily life where sport was
invented by capitalistically motivated entrepreneurs and tested and
approved by the masses of industrial society was smooth, and the evolution took place far below the life of intellect or the notice of the cote-
ries devoted to social criticism. Radical or at least rapid shifts in popular participation and culture went on so slickly that new and artificial
things such as football, basketball, high hurdles, and platform diving
seemed as if they *must* have a venerable and distinguished past.

I have claimed that England, the home of the Industrial Revolution, was the first land of sport. This is true only in a narrow way. Physical education, with which sport has had an intertwining and mutually supporting past, has other origins.

The development of sport and physical education were particular in continental Europe in that they were always regarded as too useful to be allowed haphazard development. Long before sport was noticed at all by European intellectuals, physical education in the abstract was a matter of established critical concern. European philosophers, from Niccolò Machiavelli through Martin Luther and Jean Jacques Rosseau, had included training for the body in their ideal schemes of education. Some schemes had detailed workouts for children or youths.

German pedagogues, financed by petty princelings, were the first to put varieties of these theories into practice. Johann Bernhard Basedow (1723–90), Johann Friedrich Guts Muths (1778–1839) and later, others, ran several small schools that were almost experimental laboratories for the application of theories of bodily development on small children. These educators published detailed works that were influential subsequently in much of central Europe and in Scandinavia.

Basedow and Guts Muths as physical educators are now but little remembered. The same is not so for Friedrich Ludwig Jahn (1778–1852) who, besides being an innovator in physical education and sport, is a major figure because of his work as a man of ideas. Jahn (later called *Vater* Jahn) was an innovating physical educator at the same time that he was an inspired German patriot during a period of national humiliation due to the French occupation. Jahn, himself an athlete, would not employ words of foreign origin for the exercises he proselytized among the youth—ever more of them—who came under his influence. He would not use the word "gymnastics"—already respectably in use—for his exercises, but employed instead, *turnen*, a word presumably of Teutonic origin.

What was original, convincing, and imitable about Jahn's physical education was that it was a *designed* amalgam of patriotism, community-reinforcing festivities, and exuberant bodily activities. To conservative opponents of revolutionary patriotism, Jahn's program looked dangerous—and it was. Jahn's *turnplaetze* in certain cities became assembly places for radical youths. Meetings of "turners" became opportunities to sing songs and talk about uprisings.

Sure enough, the French were expelled from Germany before the fall of Napoleon in 1815. But Jahn had new opponents. They were the conservatives of the Church and the landowning classes who wished to reinstate the regime that had existed before 1789. Jahn became ever more a leader and hero to societies of frustrated, radical students who held torchlit parades, set bonfires at the tops of hills on patriotic holidays, and even festively burned books they felt were opposed to their projects for free institutions. The murder by a radical student of a spy for the Russian government on March 23, 1819, was the signal for police throughout Germany to be unleashed at centers of subversion. The turners were obvious targets. Jahn himself was taken to the Spandau prison in Berlin where his spirit was broken. He had become torpid long before his death in 1852.

This discussion of the early days of the first *actual* schemes of organized sport (as opposed to speculative plans, which were a grand tradition in western philosophy) in Germany is not tangential to our topic. These practicing physical educationalists injected into central European political life elements that have never left it. Though sport of the kind that was becoming integrated into British and American life in the course of the nineteenth century had not yet been introduced on the continent, organized physical activity had, as sport never did, intelligent—indeed, sometimes inspired—defenders. There were debates, many of them well informed and sometimes passionate, over training routines, the use or non-use of various kinds of equipment, and whether the benefits of designed, mass physical education should be extended to children, women, the aged. There were keen debates over class exclusiveness, patriotism, and racism in the flourishing sports clubs which evolved in ways that were contemporaneously unknown in the Anglo-Saxon world—except where central European immigrants took their gymnastic societies with them, as they did to the large American cities of the Midwest.

By the later decades of the nineteenth century, the physical education movement in Germany had moved far beyond its origins in the Enlightenment and conspiratorial patriotism. The turners, in the end, had almost no influence on the achievement of German unity, which was brought about by the conservative forces of the Prussian army and the Prussian royal house. Along the way in Germany there had been some ominous discoveries of the usefulness of sports clubs. German manufacturers established internal sports clubs for their workers and found that the clubs were welcomed as a benefit and as a focus for intra-company loyalty. Designed physical training was integrated for comparable reasons into the imperial military services. The left Socialist parties organized *their* sports clubs. By the end of the century it was apparent that sports clubs could be employed as props for almost any of the new sort of collectives buttressing democratically ideological, urbanizing, industrializing society.

The technique of employing designed, purposeful sport for political ends was also an integral element in the nationalism of the Scandinavian countries and was especially effective in Czechoslovakia. Early on, the Zionists took up sport-by-design and though the Israelis have adapted the *forms* of British-American sport as propagated in the Olympic Games, the Jewish state became and remains to this day intensely committed to integrating sport in politics and ideology at all levels. An important historian of the ideology of sport has observed that sport can serve as "an advertisement" for an ideology, "indeed, virtually any ideology."[6] It should be obvious to serious observers of sports contests that the present program of Olympic sports, which are pursued at supreme levels of accomplishment in much of the world and which everywhere *look* the same, are dedicated to an array of ideological programs.

There is another insertion necessary here. I have not yet stressed that the *activities* of the two places of origin of modern sport—the British-American urban world and the sports clubs of newly modernized Germany—were quite different. Almost all central European theorists were vigorously and literarily opposed to "sport," which was correctly viewed as individualistic and commercially exploitable. The integration of Anglo-Saxon sport events into Europe was resisted and was sparse (occurring mostly among the Anglophile upper classes) until far later than most people suspect. The agency for the implantation of non-European sport was the Olympic program, which was almost entirely based on Pierre de Coubertin's lavish admiration (and ideological misreading) of British and American collegiate life. In any case, outside the British Empire and the United States, the Olympic program found little popular resonance and few effective propagators until the Nazis determined to employ the Olympic Games of 1936 for internal and external reasons. Further adaption of non-indigenous Olympic sport for ideological reasons was delayed by World War II, after which the Soviets employed induced sport with stunning effect. In recent decades imposed sport on foreign models has swept the world.[7]

A critical distinction arising is this: Where sport originated and where evolution in sports forms or presentations continue to take place—that is, in the culture that employs the language in which this essay is written—sport has almost never used, needed, or wanted intelligent defenders or critics. And few have appeared. By contrast, very early on in Germany, evolution in sport (or more accurately, physical education) was almost inconceivable apart from informed debate. All the same, debate of a fundamental sort—debates concerning the meaning, purpose, destiny or worthiness of sport came late even to Germany.

The first survey of world sport was German.[8] So was the second.[9] The third is a multi-volumed, edited German work taking essays by scholars from elsewhere and in other languages.[10] Germans have published more literature on the modern Olympic Games than all other people put together.[11] It is not idle to state here that for some time now, if the Olympic medals of the Federal (West) Germans and the Democratic (East) Germans were counted together, they would be more than those of the Soviets, the usual victors in the quadrennial games. I am not documenting athletic superiority, but rather earnestness about sport—throughout, the subject of this essay. Germans were also the first to notice the originality of English sport and to suggest reasons for this development.[12]

A further excursus can be disposed of quickly. German scholars were the earliest and remain the most productive regarding the sport of classical antiquity.[13] Moreover, Germans have been the most unselfconscious adders of pseudoclassical trappings to the ceremonies of the modern Olympic Games. Both of these developments probably result from an ancient, esthetic attachment by a few exquisitely educated Germans to classical antiquity, rather than from the ideological debates concerned with modern sport and its practical applications.

Sport criticism of the sort that might be of interest to people dissatisfied with the overwhelming bulk of journalism or escapist literature is also largely a German development—a recent one (although some notable exceptions and derivatives are indicated below). The great school of severe sports criticism, while an extension of the tradition of informed earnestness regarding planned sport and its expected consequences in Germany, could only have come about in an atmosphere of extreme press freedom and an already lively and richly disputative intellectual milieu. These conditions applied to the life of academia and publishing in West Germany as it reveled in the *Wirtschaftswunder* (economic miracle) of the 1960s.

The debaters of politics, social policy, and sport had a hot and grandly visible topic in the late 1960s: the promise of the federal government to do well in presenting the twentieth Olympic Games of the modern era, scheduled for Munich in 1972.

A burden for all Germans of our generation has been the Nazi past. Well fitted into this past were the eleventh Olympic Games in Berlin in 1936. Planning for this splendid festival had taken place when the new regime was perilously insecure. It was the occasion for the largest completed architectural complex of the Nazis. This was the first Olympic festival that offered the spectacle of an overall victory by non-American athletes. In sum the games in Berlin in 1936 were an almost seamless triumph for the new regime, both domestically and internationally.

Even more than in the imperial and Weimar regimes, sport had been intricately enmeshed in all aspects and levels of Nazi education and political indoctrination. After World War II the German consensus, which was overwhelmingly anti-Nazi, did not reject sport; Germans struggled to integrate sport into postwar schemes of education and political indoctrination. This is true of both territorial heirs of pre-1945 Germany, but most especially so of East Germany.

As the West Germans became ever more secure in their respectability, they became ever more eager to present a new festival to the world. They wished to counter the lingering impressions (certainly more vivid within Germany than without) left by the Nazi Olympics. An earnest campaign to get an Olympic festival began in 1962. In April of 1966 the International Olympic Committee awarded the 1972 games to Munich.

From the beginning almost no Germans believed the early rhetoric favoring cheap and cheerful games. The preparations were not only highly visible and enormously costly, they did not have rhetorically original or even clever defenders. The games, however, had the complete support of the financial, political (and this includes all the parties), and communications establishments.

In the meantime, this was the late sixties. Amidst the iconoclasm and revolutions of the young in the western world, there was a good deal of original derring-do among young academic intellectuals. And nowhere, perhaps, was the social criticism by academics more original or vigorous than in Germany in this period. Further, after about 1960, in West Germany every aspect of publishing was as ideologically free as it ever has been. There may never again be a place and time offering so various and so many outlets for publishing. One might imagine English and French writers alert enough to have penned the analyses that the German sport critics did, but they did not have access to so many quasi-amateur publishing houses that could eke out a commercial existence on the basis of editions of five hundred or sometimes even fewer copies. There was (and remains) another legacy of the German earnestness about sport: even today there are two solidily established mail order houses that deal with serious books on sport and physical education.

All the while there was flourishing an informal, widespread neo-Marxist critical school, with pre-war roots in the so-called "Frankfurt School."[14] The German critical school was acquainted with and was sometimes enthusiastic about the work of the American social critic, David McClelland, and his followers, who were investigating what they called "the achievement principle" in capitalistic society.

The initial monument was a small book by Bero Rigauer, a young sociologist. It had the chilling title, *Sport und Arbeit,* and a particularly irreverent opening paragraph, much of which I present (in Guttmann's translation) below.

> Sports are not an autonomous system of behavior; they appear along with numerous other social developments whose origins lie in early-capitalist bourgeois society. Although sports have constituted a specific realm of social behavior, they remain embedded in interdependent social processes which account for their fundamental characteristics—discipline, authority, competition, achievement, goal-oriented rationality, organization, and bureaucratization, to name but a few. In modern industrial society, certain techniques of productive work have become such dominant models of conduct that they impose their norms even upon so-called leisure-time activities. Sports have not been able to escape this imposition of norms.[15]

The book goes on in this fashion. What made Rigauer's essay so especially striking is that it is a fundamental analysis of modern sport everywhere—not just in the Federal Republic which was so absorbed in the costly preparations for the games mentioned above.

Less substantial, but nevertheless stirring to read, was Gerhard Vinnai's *Fussballsport als Ideologie* (Frankfurt: Europaeische, 1970).[16] Another book, a hard look at the origins of the modern Olympic Games and a particularly unsympathetic examination of the theoretical writings of the originating saint of the Olympics, Pierre de Coubertin, is Ulrike Prokop's *Soziologie der olympischen Spiele* (Munich: Carl Hanser, 1971). These were the early books that released more neo-Marxists such as Sven Gueldenpfenning, Renate Pfister, Wilhelm Hopf, and others.

These left critics raised, possibly permanently, the whole level of consideration that must henceforth be employed when we examine sport. There were others, not necessarily of the left and not necessarily young academics, who wrote brilliantly and analytically on sport in the early seventies. Some of these were Hans Lenk, Ommo Gruppe, Christian Graf von Krokow, and Arnd Krueger. Their works are completely cited in the notes to Guttmann's introduction to Rigauer, cited above.

Speaking as a cultural historian and as one who must confess intellectual debts, I feel that the star whose work will longest remain valuable was Henning Eichberg. Eichberg was young and was part of an institute in Stuttgart that was investigating the historical and psychological bases of social thought. This was while the debates of the Munich preparations were especially lively. Eichberg published two particularly novel historical articles and then a book.[17]

Eichberg then clinched it with another book-length essay that deals only partly with sport. This last, splendid work also discusses dance, military fortifications, and many other topics to show the profound shifts in the way the domininant and opinion making classes of Europe viewed time and space in the later eighteenth century. Essential background for future work on modern sport is Eichberg's *Leistung, Spannung, Geschwindigkeit* (Stuttgart: Klett-Cotta, 1978). Eichberg's work is marred by a neglect of English and American sociological writing—much of which would surely buttress his claims. Nonetheless, all of this cited work and more has been enormously emboldening to me and to Allen Guttmann.

This eruption of sports critical literature may have been essentially a reaction to the preoccupations in German cultural circles with the Munich games, which, except for the calamity of the atrocity committed by Palestinian outlaws against the Israeli team, went on and were concluded almost according to plan.[18]

Though a theoretical basis was established, the energy of these critics passed to other things after 1972 as the sports scene and the disputatious political scene were more or less normalized in the ever richer and more secure Federal Republic. Rigauer subsequently wrote little about sport. Eichberg, who moved on to other things, now repeats himself when he writes about sport. It might be the case that what there is original to be said about the significance of modern sport was so splendidly presented (I refer my readers to the sentences of Rigauer above) that there is not much more to say. Nonetheless, this movement has left us its literary monuments and has not been surpassed in originality, rigor, or bravery. It is to the discredit of the sports world everywhere that this corpus of work is, after all this time, only beginning to be known where German is not employed with ease.

Critical American writing on sport includes some sound work that has appeared apart from the German tradition. Yet little of this work is based on any general social-critical theory—whether radical Marxist or conservative-Christian; rather, it is merely the product of the analysts' raw energy, intelligence, and cynicism. Earnest sports criticism in the American tradition seems to be merely angry, not theoretical.

Many of us treasure, for example, Robert Lipsyte's *Sportsworld: An American Dreamland* (New York: Quadrangle, 1975, 292 pp.). Lipsyte offered and I have kept for my own use some neologisms such as the book's title, and "manchat," as well as lot of funny phrases and the Lipsyte character "Charlie Lumpenfan." However, the book is a bitter reaction, the end product of fourteen years of (relatively) self-controlled output as a sports columnist for the *New York Times*. It is a bilious outburst against the conventions of American media reporting. Lipsyte tells us that sunny reporting on the stars of professional and collegiate sport is hypocritical, and is paralyzed by the cretinous and inflexible forms of sports reportage. Lipsyte has since moved on to other things— as have other bitter and inspired Americans who began their careers writing about sport, notably Ring Lardner and Paul Gallico.

A critic whose contribution will be less durable, but who provides a transition to a subsequent leading character in this essay, is Leonard Shecter (1926–74), another veteran of New York daily sports journalism. In his later days and the last days of the weekly newsmagazine, *Look,* Schecter was its sports editor. Though cynical and sickly, this tough bird shared in the iconoclasm of the 1960s, publishing *The Jocks* (New York: Bobbs-Merrill) in 1969. My paperback edition (New York: Paperback Library, 1970, 291+ pp.) has the front page blurb, "The book that takes the halo off sports heroes." This wholesome tirade is funny and is filled with memorable phrases—one of the best of which is, "Sportswriters—you can buy them with a steak."

I am quite deliberately bringing this book up not only because it is a delight to read, but because it merits some monumentalization as an example of rugged criticism where criticism of any kind is rare. Shecter seems to have pulled up all the in-phrases and secret lore of decades of tale collecting among professional peers, and his survey is confined almost entirely to American athletes who were worthy of media attention in his days. There is no wider scope.

One of Shecter's finds as an editor of *Look* was Jack Scott, who merits closer attention as the American sports critic who has come closest to producing a fundamental analysis and censure of modern sport. Jack Scott went to Stanford University on an athletic scholarship. Due to some injuries, his career there was undistinguished athletically as well as academically. He eventually got a degree at Syracuse University. He then entered the University of California at Berkeley in 1968. These were the days when Berkeley was a birthplace and epicenter for the era's protest movements. As a graduate student in the physical education department, Jack began modestly and then enthusiastically to go at the institutions of collegiate sport. His critique fit into the general iconoclasm of the times.

Through a small press in Berkeley, he published a pasted-together collection of some of his articles that had appeared in *Track and Field News,* a couple of essays by others, and some reprinted newspaper clippings, under the title that summarized his position—*Athletics for Athletes* (Oakland, California: Other Ways Press, 1969, 111 pp.). This was picked up by Leonard Shecter who gave Jack some space on the other coast in the nationally distributed *Look.* Thereafter, Jack was in the news a lot. He was readily accessible to young sports writers, who found him full of lively sixties rhetoric at the other end of the long distance phone line. Interviews appeared everywhere and Jack collected photocopies of the newsprint columns which he gave out readily to those who might want to employ them.

Jack was marvelous copy. Though balding, he was still young and wiry. He and his wife, Micki, had good ears for absorbing the stories of dissident college athletes, some of whom traveled great distances to sit at their feet in the couple's small house in Oakland. Jack grandly declared that he was the director of the "Institute for the Study of Sport and Society," which had his domestic address. Jack and Micki were available for long, intensely conversational runs in the neighborhood and elsewhere in the Bay Area. People were invited to come to assemblies of the "institute" in order to "rap." This writer was one of many who lounged around on the floor of Jack's living room while ex-jocks, many in hippie drag, waved their hands in the air complaining about the present age. We pulled beers from six-packs and blew grass. I was, at the time, a researcher at the conservative Hoover Library in Palo Alto. It was fun.

During the winter of 1970, the University of California employed Jack to teach a course on the role of athletics in higher education and let him say what he wished to some four hundred registered students. By this time Scott had attracted allies. One was Harry Edwards, a big man who attempted in 1968 with his "Olympic Project for Human Rights" to arrange for a boycott of the games scheduled for Mexico City in that year. Edwards was a leader of the American runners who so scandalized Olympic officials in Mexico by mildly altering the prescribed behavior at victory ceremonies to make what ever afterwards has been called a "black power protest." Edwards also began a career at Berkeley.

Though he wrote little for them, Jack also had for several years the title of sports editor of the high-profile social-critical magazine, *Ramparts*. One of the great troubles of Jack Scott was the writing up of original material. If one had a corresponding relationship with him— and I did—the information that he sent out was usually the photocopied editorials that he had inspired in young sports writers elsewhere. His opus, a book published in 1971 by the Free Press with the provocative title, *The Athletic Revolution* (242 pp.), actually includes a lot of material by other people.

This book merits some examination as a monument to the brief popular age of American sports criticism. The book is dedicated "To the many individuals whose courage and commitment are helping to make the athletic revolution," and quotes at the beginning Bernadette Devlin, who said, "We were born into an unjust system; we are not prepared to grow old with it." In a bold hand the author wrote in my personal copy, "For Dick, a fellow struggler. With warm regards, Jack Scott."

The first chapter uses some of Jack's prose, but it is mostly a short narrative by Sylvester Hodges, a small, remarkably handsome black man and, for a while, one of the best wrestlers in the NCAA college division. Hodges had just been barred from competition because he had refused to obey a coaches' rule that individuals not have "facial hair below the middle of the ear lobe." Hodges wanted to keep the tiny mustache that he had worn when he wrestled for three years in the army. The memoir would be risible and conceivably heroic, if it were not pathetic: the incident marked the end of a happy athlete's sporting career. In a couple of italicized paragraphs after the wrestler's tale, Jack Scott tells us that in a poll of 510 college wrestling coaches about the "no hair" rule, 490 voted to retain it.

Another chapter contains excerpts from one of the first substantial products of the group (membership varied) of disenchanted athletes who made up the institute. Dave Meggyesy had been a college football player at Syracuse University and then for seven years more was a linebacker with the St. Louis Cardinals. He dropped out and, encouraged and helped by Jack, spilled the beans. Meggyesy's book, *Out of their League* (Berkeley: Ramparts Presss, 1970, 257 pp.) told a story of corruption and disillusionment. It was intended to be one of many such revelations out of Jack Scott's stable of dissentniks. Meggyesy's book may be one of the first or at least the most corrosively critical of the steady march of books since that time that reveal just how difficult it is to maintain the pace of hypocrisy and discipline in the football business. What makes *Out of their League* so dated is all that sixties rhetoric of anger against the present and, conversely, optimism about the future.

The Athletic Revolution also contained some good chapters on the "the revolt of the Black athlete" which were heavily dependent upon the agitation of Harry Edwards, at the time an untenured assistant professor in the sociology department at the University of California. Jack went after the amateur rule in intercollegiate athletics; drugs; the role of alumni in collegiate athletic programs; and he even made some of the first, vigorous statements proposing equal treatment for women in all sports. The outrage in the book and the objects of it no longer seem unusual. All of the topics were to remain in the news subsequently. What makes Jack Scott interesting is that his views were integrated into a general criticism of society as it was.

My little survey has not communicated how much fun all this was. Jack was mischievously provocative. A certain Stan Goldberg, at the time ranked third nationally in the college decathlon, had announced before the NCAA Track and Field Championships in 1970 that he planned to make some sort of peaceful protest against the killings of students at Kent State University. He was forthwith kicked off the team at the University of Kansas and had his athletic scholarship cancelled. Jack made a lot of telephone calls and saw to it that Goldberg was appointed "Minister of Sport and Physical Education" for a certain Youth International Party. Of course this got to all the papers. Jack rushed to defend athletes who were barred from competition for the wearing of long hair or bandanas. He was ironically pleased that Dee Andros, the head football coach at Oregon State, after dismissing a black player for wearing a goatee during the off season, allowed himself to be quoted: "My policies haven't changed in twenty years."

Jack Scott employed the always hot issue of sexual inversion. In print and in public confrontations he would state that the relationship between athlete and coach was in essence exploitive and homosexual. Whole phalanxes of professionals whose stance had always been stridently butch became furiously riled and declarative. Jack became yet more famous. He collected photocopies from young reporters who had interviewed offended coaches on this issue, written down what they had said, and then phoned him to see what he had to say in response.

Scott got job offers. He signed papers accepting an assistant professorship at the University of Washington. In those days academic administrators would do strange things in order to get "exposure"—a desirable thing, it seemed—and Jack promised a lot of it. Pressure from the athletic department then caused the appointment to be cancelled and Jack sued for $350,000. He settled for less.

In 1973 Jack Scott and his institute settled at Oberlin College in northern Ohio where he was the new director of athletics and physical education. Tommie Smith, a 1968 gold medal winner in Mexico and the center of the "black power" demonstrations there, was named assistant director. Paul Hoch, a vociferous self-proclaimed Marxist who published a book with the title *Rip Off the Big Game* (New York: Doubleday, 1972, 222 pp.) was made assistant professor of physical education. Jack hired Leslie Rudolph, a great All-American swimmer, as a coach, and more women turned out for the swim team than men had done for the team the year before. Jack was moving fast. Reporters and television crews hung around pastoral Oberlin. Then, at first slowly but with rapidly increasing speed, the whole undertaking collapsed. The president of Oberlin who had allowed Scott such sphere was let go, and it was clear that Jack was far too much even for experimental Oberlin, which had long been famous for its amalgamation of excellence and liberty.

It is giving Jack Scott too much credit to say that he initiated a lot of the reform movements that now swirl about (without reforming much) in American collegiate and professional sport. Sport has certainly been integrated into feminism, increasing female participation, support, and popular coverage. There is now almost a genre of tell-it-all-afterwards literature in collegiate and professional football (though much less so in other sports). As drug abuse in sport has become more widespread and deadly, the organized revulsion against it has moved way beyond Jack's carping about amphetamines and pain killers and has entered the media mainstream.

There are, in fact, many worthwhile and legitimate currents of the sports criticism of the present that may be traceable to the corrosive social criticism of the late sixties and seventies and, if we wish to be generous, to Jack Scott's role as a focus for it all. However, what is still missing from the sports scene and the social-critical scene alike is an amalgamation that would, in turn, be integrated into a fundamental theoretical position. Even Jack Scott, who liked to be called a "Marxist" and reveled in the appellation "revolutionary," was really, in the end, another of the energetic hustlers who have made their way and, in the course of things, altered the rich and steadily creative mixture that has been and remains American sport.

Scott had been far from the public eye for some time. He had a brief emergence when it was revealed that he had played a large role in the Patty Hearst case, using some connections with her kidnappers to hang around them. He took the poor girl, in disguise, across the U.S. a couple of times and hid her in "safe houses." He had hoped to write a financially rewarding book about the case. Almost all of the people around Scott were likewise little heard from again. An exception is Harry Edwards, who has continued to talk and write (rather repetitiously, it seems) on the victimization of the black athlete.[19] Edwards is on TV regularly and is now a high official in league baseball administration.

The quality of serious writing on sport by Americans continues to improve. *The Journal of Sport History*, which began publication in 1974 as an organ for the release of work by American physical educationalists, is now a good academic periodical, like many others. There is a fine survey of American sport by Benjamin G. Rader, *American Sports* (Englewood Cliffs: Prentice-Hall, 1983, 376 pp.). I do not wish to demean the more-than-respectable scholarship being done now by a lot of young American sports historians, but they seem too often stuck on laboring over specific periods in particular American cities, or biographies of baseball players and boxers. Too many of them dwell, as American writers on sport at all levels always have, on baseball.

Almost all American writing about sport is about American sport. Similarly and comparably, almost all Canadian writing about sport is about Canadian sport. This holds true for Australia as well.

There is some optimism among American sports scholars now as scouts for commercial and university presses seek respectable work on sport. Books on sport sell. But we could be more sanguine about the future if some of this published material were more than merely respectable, and if it were based on comprehensive theoretical positions regarding society as a whole and the role that a critical intellectual should play in it.

There is a subsection of American intellectual life in which the level of sports criticism is very high and the number of fans rather low. This material does not fit in the rubric described above. The leader is Allen Guttmann, a professor of American studies at Amherst College. Guttmann in the early chapters of his book, *From Ritual to Record*,[20] has given as vigorous and convincing a statement as we are likely to see of the modernists' view that sport as we know it is something new under the sun. Characteristically, Guttmann's biography of Avery Brundage (*The Games Must Go On* [New York: Columbia University

Press, 1984, 317 pp.]) stresses his subject's role in European and Latin American affairs. Guttmann's eccentrically focused survey of sport from the beginning, his *Sports Spectators* (New York: Columbia University Press, 1986, 236 pp.) eclectically uses research or speculation from a grand range of disciplines and languages. Guttmann is extravagantly well read and alert. His recent interpretive survey of American sport, *A Whole New Ball Game* (Chapel Hill: University of North Carolina Press, 1988, 233 pp.), is so richly analytical that the study of American sport cannot be the same after this. We already know that Guttmann's scheduled book on women in sport will also set new standards in the English-speaking world.

Another American scholar who has done splendid work based on investigation in many areas and languages is John M. Hoberman. His *Sport and Political Ideology*[21] deals with an immense variety of literary sources and (amazing!) almost ignores America. Hoberman's *The Olympic Crisis: Sports, Politics and the Moral Order* (New Rochelle: Caratzas, 1986, 220 pp.) is a many-sided exposé and takes strong positions on many aspects of Olympism.

It is correct to say that Guttmann, Hoberman and even myself are publicly honest about our dependence on the German tradition, particularly the neo-Marxist critical school of the late sixties and early seventies. We remain petulant that so many of our colleagues elsewhere in the world continue to labor on without it.

Perhaps one of the noblest expenditures of labor on the part of the increasingly self-conscious school of American sports-critical studies would be to translate Rigauer, von Krockow, Eichberg, and perhaps a half-dozen others. This would accelerate the pace at which sports studies continue to improve.

NOTES

1. I refer here to a posited "Eichberg-Guttmann-Mandell" thesis regarding the integration of modern sport in modern life. Works that are central in this thesis will be cited below. An item in this debate is the sports record. One can look at my article on this: "The Invention of the Sports Record," *Stadion* (Cologne) 2, no. 2 (1976), 250–64. A group of European (mostly) and American scholars are now planning a collective work to demonstrate that sport records existed in such places as Egypt and pre-Meijei Japan and intend thereby to undermine the thesis named above: J. M. Carter and A. Krueger, ed.,

Ritual and Record: Sports Quantification in Pre-Industrial Societies (Westport, Conn.: Greenwood Press, forthcoming).

2. See the early chapters of his *From Ritual to Record* (New York: Columbia University Press, 1978). There is a German translation.

3. See my *Sport: A Cultural History* (New York: Columbia University Press, 1984), particularly chapters VII and VIII. (There are German, Spanish, and Italian translations.)

4. Published in English (New York: Harper and Row, 1981–84). First published in Paris in 1979. There are editions in other languages.

5. A salient and convincing essay with fine bibliographical notes is by David S. Landes: *Prometheus Unbound: Technological Change and Industrial Development in Western Europe from 1750 to the Present* (Cambridge: Cambridge University Press, 1969).

6. John M. Hoberman, *Sport and Political Ideology* (Austin: University of Texas Press, 1984), p. 1. It is keenly significant that Hoberman in this instant classic ignores American sport because "any attempt to correlate the values embodied in American sport with ideological positions will be difficult, simply because American sport, its 'ideological' content notwithstanding, has no official position" (p. 2). Hoberman here fortifies a distinction that will loom large in the rest of this paper.

7. I sometimes hike in the remote Guatemalan highlands. Every village has a football field. In Guatemala I have run ten-kilometer races. The two newspapers of large circulation have lots of sports news including dispatches from the wire services describing major team confrontations or records set internationally.

8. G. A. E. Bogeng, *Geschichte des Sports all Voelker and Zeiten* (Leipzig: E. S. Seemann, 1926), 2 vols.

9. Carl Diem, *Weltgeschichte des Sports* (Stuttgart: Cotta, first edition, 1960), 1,224 pp. There is a Spanish translation.

10. See Horst Ueberhorst, ed. *Geschichte der Leibesuebungen* (Berlin: Bartels und Wernitz, 1972+). Scheduled for eight volumes; seven have been published.

11. The best survey, still, is Walter Umminger, *Die olympischen Spiele der Neuzeit* (Dortmund: Olympischer Sportverlag, 1967). A work that is splendid for its bibliographical completeness is Hans Lenk, *Werte, Ziele, Wirklichkeit der modernen olympischen Spiele* (Stuttgart: Hofmann, 1964 ["Verbesserte Auflage," 1972]).

12. See Herbert Schoeffler, *England, das Land des Sports: Eine kultur-soziologische Erklaerung* (Leipzig: Tauchnitz, 1935). Much of the analysis of Schoeffler's essay is based on the documents assembled by his dissertation student. See Maria Kloeren's *Sport und Rekord: Untersuchungen zum England des sechszehnten bis achtzehnten Jahrhunderts* ("Koelner anglistische Arbeiten") (Leipzig: Tauchnitz, 1935); Johnson reprints reissued this in New York in 1966. Another early essay is U. Hirn, *Ursprung und Wesen des Sports* (Berlin: Weidmannsche, 1936). It is only very recently that Englishmen have approached the analytical profundity of these works. One can consult Dennis Brailsford, *Sport and Society: Elizabeth to Anne* (London: Routledge, 1969). It is a pleasure to claim that the work of one British scholar (who, it must be stated, is much indebted to the German social critic, Norbert Elias) is right up to the highest standards of investigation and analysis of the Germans. For fine, critical sport history one can read (very likely with pleasure) the work of Eric Dunning, *Barbarians, Gentlemen and Players: A Sociological Study of the Development of Rugby Football* (New York: New York University Press, 1979).

13. I have already written on this in "The Modern Olympic Games: A Bibliographical Essay," *Sportwissenschaft* 6, no. 1 (1976): 89–98.

14. A good discussion of the intellectual roots of this is in the introduction (pp. vii–xxxiv) by Allen Guttmann to his translation, *Sport and Work* (New York: Columbia University Press, 1981) of Bero Rigauer's *Sport und Arbeit*.

15. First published, Frankfurt: Suhrkamp, 1969. A second edition with a "Nachwort" (Afterword) was published in 1979.

16. There were clumsy English and Spanish translations.

17. "Auf Zoll und Quintlein," *Archiv fuer Kulturgeschichte* 56 (1974): 141–76; "Der Beginn des modernen Leistens," *Sportwissenschaft* 4 (1974): 21–48; *Der Weg des Sports in die industrielle Zivilisation* (Baden-Baden: Nomos, 1974). There was a second printing in 1979 with a "Nachwort."

18. I plan soon to publish a book that will discuss the integration of the Munich Olympics in Federal German public life. I will stress the successful aspects of this critically placed festival.

19. See, for example, his *Revolt of the Black Athlete* (New York: Free Press, 1969) and *The Struggle that Must Be* (New York: Macmillan, 1980).

20. See note 2.

21. See note 6.

ALLEN GUTTMANN

Eros and Sport

AMONG those of us in love with sports, the topic "eros and sport" is taboo. Violations of the taboo are liable to be met with expressions of anger. When the mechanisms of denial with which we protect ourselves from our own emotions work to perfection, assertions about the relationship between sport and eros are likely to be deflected by smiles of condescension rather than by hoots of derision or the resort to physical expressions of disagreement. The strangest aspect of the taboo is that the embarrassed denials are stammered by those who normally affirm the joy of sports. Those who, on the other hand, have been negative about sports have repeatedly drawn indignant attention to the erotic element. Their exasperated insistence that sports are an occasion for erotic indulgence have usually been countered by self-deceptive remarks about fresh air and good fun. In response to the accusation of voyeurism, the spectators enamored of sports have proclaimed their appreciation of "thrills and spills" and "all the moves" (except the erotic ones).

Although YMCA workers, physical educators, and coaches have propagated the modern myth that a heated contest and a cold shower diminish or divert adolescent sexuality, clerical critics of sports since the days of St. Augustine have maintained the opposite. They allege that sports can sexually arouse participants and spectators alike. It is not accidental that physical education classes have continued to segregate boys from girls long after coeducational math and music are taken for granted. In the nineteenth century, a number of medical experts complained that the craze for the bicycle was a thinly disguised desire for masturbation. In the twentieth century, right wing religious leaders have thundered their anathemas against female gymnasts who perform before mixed audiences. At the other end of the political spectrum, neo-Marxist critics have condemned sports because they enhance a woman's sexual attractiveness and thus increase what they call her "erotic ex-change-value."[1] Some radical feminists have agreed with them.

Have the critics right and left been misguided? Not completely. Rather than dismissing their complaints as prurient or narrow-minded, we should ask ourselves a question: How much *does* eros have to do with our human response to sports as participants and as spectators? Before venturing an answer, I need to clarify some concepts.

Sports I define as I have in my previous work: autotelic physical contests. Eros is a much more problematic concept. If one defines the term broadly in the manner of Sigmund Freud in such late works as *Civilization and Its Discontents* (1930), it becomes much more than a desire for sexual union. Its scope enlarges until it becomes all that makes for life rather than death. It becomes the mighty opposite of thanatos. In fact, Freud may have invented the notion of thanatos in order to deflect criticism that his conception of eros left no room for any other drive. In this extended Freudian sense of the concept, sports and every other form of human prowess are manifestations of eros.

It is more useful, however, to define eros more narrowly as that force or drive (*Trieb*) that begins with a sense of physical attraction and aims at sexual fulfillment. It is important to understand the word "attraction" in its literal sense—to attract is to pull towards; to say that someone is attractive is to admit that one feels physically drawn towards that person. In this narrower sense, eros is synonymous with what Freud in such early works as *Three Essays on Sexual Theory* (1905) referred to as "libido." In fact, Freud was quite explicit on the identity of eros and libido in *Group Psychology and the Analysis of the Ego* (1921), where he scornfully ridiculed those who timidly prefer the genteel Greek term eros to the clinical expression libido and the ordinary German word *Liebe*. Despite Freud's sarcasm, eros seems the best word to describe the power of sexual attraction. Libido, although it is the Latin word used by St. Augustine, now seems *too* clinical; "love" suggests too much spirituality. Whatever one thinks of Freud's terminology, one should take seriously Freud's remark that libido, which many psychologists had simply assumed to be a physiological given, is as worthy of investigation as the libido's object. "The profoundest difference," he wrote, "between the love-life of the ancient world and our own lies in the fact that antiquity placed the accent on the impulse, we on its object."[2] The insight was profound. Freud returned the emphasis to where it had been in antiquity, on the impulse.

Enough on terminology. In order to bring some further clarity into the murk that surrounds discussions of sport and eros, we need to consider the responses of both the spectator and the participant. In each case, we can ask about responses to both the athlete and the athletic performance. In the case of the participant, there is an additional dimension—the athlete's awareness of the spectator and the resultant tendency to transform play into display.[3]

Let us begin with the spectators' response to the athlete rather than with their response to the athletic performance. Greek sculptors carved and cast statues of Olympic victors; modern television advertisers pay Olympians to endorse their products. The Greeks, however, were more candid about the appeals of the human body than we have tended to be. Although it is surely an exaggeration to claim, as some historians have, that Greek men preferred homosexual to heterosexual love, there is no reason to doubt that the youthful male body was considered beautiful and that erotic relationships between an older and a younger man were socially acceptable. They were, indeed, idealized as a form of pedagogy.

Sports were a central part of the relationship. K. J. Dover, the recognized authority on Greek homosexuality, remarks that "athletic success seems to have been a powerful stimulus to . . . potential lovers."[4] In *Peace*, the comic playwright Aristophanes comments offhandedly that he "never went off to make love to the boys in the schools of athletic display" (ll. 762–63). Several millenia later, the stimulus remains operative. Edgar Friedenberg, the American sociologist, has acknowledged the excitement he feels at the sight of young boys playing and has affirmed the presence of "a strong and pervasive erotic strain in the human response to athletic spectacles."[5] If all of us are attracted to beautiful men as well as to beautiful women, which is a psychoanalytic commonplace, then there may be an answer to Brian Stoddart's objection that sexuality cannot be much of a factor in spectatorship because men do not seem as interested in women's sports as women are in men's. It may be that the sexuality is there—in sublimated form.[6] Needless to say, the erotic strain occurs in heterosexual forms as well.

In many pre-literate societies sports are part of the *rites de passage* from childhood to manhood or womanhood. For centuries, perhaps for millenia, the pubescent boys and girls of Africa have wrestled as part of their ritual initiation into adulthood. The entire village gathered to celebrate such moments of communal liminality. Among the Diola of Gambia, for instance, adolescent boys and girls wrestled (but not against one another) and the male champion was often married to his female counterpart. Among the Yala of Nigeria and the Njabi of the Congo, the adolescent boys and girls wrestled one another.[7] The male Nuba of the Sudan, stunningly photographed by Leni Riefenstahl in *The Last of the Nuba* (New York: Harper & Row, 1974), wrestled one another to attest their virility, to enhance the prestige of their villages, to please the gods, and to attract the amorous attentions of the maidens who watched the contests in a state of excited anticipation. (There is, incidentally, no more erotic sports film than Riefenstahl's famed *Olympia* [1938], a cinematic declaration of love if ever there was one.)

Although wrestling, with its surface similarity to sexual union, has always been the sport most directly associated with primitive fertility ritual, other sports have also functioned to announce and celebrate physical maturation. In Papua New Guinea, for example, anthropologists have observed a ritual tug-of-war, men against women, performed by moonlight to increase the fertility of nature and of humankind.[8] The ceremonial stickball games of the North American Indians, played by women as well as by men, seem also to have been courtship or fertility rituals.[9]

The civilizations of classical antiquity were admirably conscious of the erotic associations of sports, and admirably without hypocrisy. Although men's sports played an enormously important role in Greek culture as in ours, women's sports were relatively unimportant—except in the form of ritual. Recent excavations at Brauron near Athens have unearthed evidence of races run by naked adolescent girls as part of their prenuptial initiation into mature womanhood.[10] What the Athenian girls did once in their lives, Spartan girls did as part of their daily routine. The Spartans were notorious in the eyes of other Greeks because girls as well as boys were required regularly to train as athletes and to compete in public. The motivation was political and eugenic—to produce vigorous mothers and thus to engender the healthy boys required by a military state. The historian Xenophon, who was an admirer of Spartan customs, wrote: "These public processions of the maidens and their appearing naked in their exercises and dancings, were incitements to marriage, operating upon the young with the rigor of certainty, as Plato says, of love if not of mathematics."[11] The word "love" might better have been left untranslated—as "eros." Commenting on Spartan practices, a modern classicist agrees that the function of the races and processions was erotic; they demonstrated the eugenic fitness of the adolescent girls and acted "to stimulate the young [male] spectators to matrimony."[12]

Centuries later, the Roman poet Propertius, known for his erotic verses, was unrestrained and almost absurdly lyrical about these Spartan girls:

> I much admire the Spartan wrestling schools,
> but most of all I like the women's rules:
> for girls and men can wrestle in the nude
> (the Spartans think such exercise is good);
> naked they throw the ball too fast to catch,
> and steer the creaking hoop in the bowling match,
> stand waiting, grimed with dust, for the starting gun,
> and bear the brunt of the Pancration,
> put boxing gloves on hands so soft and fair,
> and whirl the heavy discus through the air,
> gallop the circuit, helmets on their brow,
> buckling a sword to thighs as white as snow;
> with hoar-frost on their hair, they join the chase
> as the hounds of Sparta climb Taygetus,
> like Amazons, breasts naked to the fray,
> who bathed in Pontic streams at the end of day,
> like Helen training on Eurotas' sands
> with nipples bare and weapons in their hands,
> while boxer, horseman, champions to be,
> her brothers watched, and did not blush to see.[13]

Needless to say, Propertius relied more on his febrile imagination than upon the historical record, but who is to say that his was the only imagination overheated by the thought of muscular, bellicose, nubile physicality?

The Roman satirist Juvenal agreed with his predecessor on the associations of eros and sports, but he condemned rather than celebrated them. He vituperated aristocratic Roman women who found athletes sexually irresistible. In Juvenal's *Satires*, a senator's wife is said to have thought gladiators "look better than any Adonis."[14] Archeological evidence from Pompeii suggests that Juvenal was a keen observer of Roman customs. In the courtyard of the palaestra in Pompeii, archeologists found the skeleton of a woman who seems to have let the love ignited by a gladiator overcome her fears of volcanic eruption.[15]

The medieval tournament may seem far removed from the domain of eros, but the relationship between feats of arms and the code of courtly love was strikingly direct. The medieval tournament began in the twelfth century as a deadly free-for-all combat between teams of armored warriors who assaulted each other with a passion suggesting thanatos rather than eros, but the sport evolved over a period of four hundred years and underwent what the German sociologist Norbert Elias has referred to as a "civilizing process."[16]

By the fifteenth century, the frequently deadly mock battles had become theatrical performances full of allegorical pageantry. The tournament appeared in fictional form in the romances of Chrétien de Troyes, and the romance—with all the attendant fol-de-rol of courtly love—influenced the subsequent development of the tournament. The conventions of the late medieval tournament called for a love-smitten knight to knot his beloved's scarf around the tip of his blunted lance and to display his military prowess as a means to win her favor. Around the joust there exfoliated a fantastic make-believe world of giants, dwarfs, magicians, enchanted damsels, and dutiful unicorns that laid their heads in ladies' laps. When the tournament took the popular form of the *Table Ronde,* the participants masqueraded as Lancelot and Guinevere or as Tristan and Isolde. While the military and political functions of the tournament never wholly disappeared, the erotic function—suitably conventionalized—became increasingly prominent.[17]

The relationship between sport and eros appeared in crasser form at the other end of the social hierarchy. While lords and ladies played at courtly love, prostitutes competed in the footraces that were a regular feature of medieval and Renaissance fairs and carnivals. Ferrara, Florence, and a number of other Italian cities had such races. In 1501, Pope Alexander VI, a member of the Borgia family and obviously no spoilsport, hosted a prostitutes' race at Saint Peter's basilica in Rome. Such contests were also common north of the Alps. Sometimes the *gemeine Weiber* ran in the same race with their untainted sisters, as they did in Noerdlingen in 1442, and sometimes the fallen women had the field to themselves, as they did in Augsburg in 1452. Commenting on the carnival-time contests in Basel, one historian remarks that the lightly clad prostitutes were exemplars of *Liebesuebungen* rather than *Leibesuebungen* ("exercises in love" rather than "exercises of the body").[18]

Is twentieth-century behavior all that different from ancient antics? In our own time, it is common knowledge that American baseball players are beleaguered by erotically dazzled young women known as "baseball Annies." It is common to refer to young male athletes as "studs." I assume that this locution acknowledges a connection between eros and sports. Johnny Weismuller is a splendid example as well as a splendid specimen. The Olympic swimmer was chosen to play the role of Tarzan because the producers wanted someone with sex appeal. The whole nature of women's gymnastics changed in the 1980s when beautiful young women like Ludmilla Turescheva and Nelli Kim were replaced by tiny preadolescent children. Turescheva, a hauntingly beautiful woman, can be admired in David Wolpers' *Visions of Eight*, a documentary film about the 1972 Olympic Games, where her performance on the uneven parallel bars is the high point of the section entitled "The Women."

Male and female athletes are not unaware of their physical attractiveness. "Broadway Joe" Namath marketed his sex appeal almost as successfully as he sold his quarterbacking skills. "Men," remarked female pentathlete Jane Frederick, "go cuckoo for me."[19] Noting that sex and sports are both forms of physical expression, runner Lynda Huey asks, "How can anyone want anyone but an athlete?"[20] Florence "Flo-Jo" Griffith-Joyner is another example of a stellar athlete presenting herself as a source of erotic delight. *Winning Women* is a marvelously illustrated book of photographs by Tony Duffy, who says in the introduction, "I have always enjoyed taking photos of female athletes. . . . They've got natural grace and tend to show their emotions more than the men. As a result, they're often more fun to watch."[21] Is it possible that Duffy has resorted to euphemism? Further examples are surely unnecessary, but it is important to emphasize the obvious fact that not all athletes are physically attractive and that physical attractiveness is certainly not the only reason for the spectator's admiration of the athlete as an athlete.

There is also the performance. The difficulty, of course, is that we can no more separate the dancer from the dance than could William

Butler Yeats. Still, the Dionysian language we use to describe sports performances is suggestive. Fans are thrilled, excited, frenzied. It would be foolish to claim that the spectator's response to physical prowess invariably has an erotic component, but it is worth recalling that Freud's theory of sadism and masochism posits a sexual origin for both responses.[22] If one credits his theory, which seems a plausible one, then one must acknowledge the existence of an erotic element in a wide variety of combat sports.

If, however, one rejects Freud's analysis of sadism and masochism and, consequently, denies the existence of an erotic component in the spectators' thrilled reactions to the brutal performances of professional boxers, what can one say about the sports occupying the other end of the spectrum? How can anyone deny that eros plays a part in the so-called "aesthetic" sports—gymnastics, figure skating, surfing, diving, and synchronized swimming? The spectator who felt no erotic pleasure at the sight of Katerina Witt's dance to the music of *Carmen* at the 1988 Winter Olympics must have had a heart as cold as the ice she skated on.

Furthermore, if art is, as Freud argued, a sublimation of sexual energies, is it farfetched to imagine an erotic component in our response to art? Skeptics may be tempted to insist at this point that there is a difference between aesthetic and erotic responses to the human body. Indeed there is, but Kenneth Clark should be cited on this point: "No nude, however abstract, should fail to arouse in the spectator some vestige of erotic feeling, even though it be only the faintest shadow— and if it does not do so, it is bad art and false morals."[23] If one takes seriously the assumptions that motivated twentieth-century British theatrical censors to accept motionless nudes upon the stage but to ban nudes in motion as lascivious and lewd, then it follows that the performances of gymnasts and divers and skaters might well arouse a spectator more than their bodies at rest.

When we turn from the spectators to the participants, the analysis becomes more complicated. How does the athlete respond to his or her own body? Ulrich Dix and other neo-Marxist critics of sports have published blanket assertions to the effect that athletes are exhibitionistic victims of their own narcissism, men and women whose libido is directed at their own bodies. Like Otto Fenichel in *The Psychoanalytic Theory of Neurosis* (New York: W. W. Norton & Co., 1945), Dix assumes that athletes' narcissism and exhibitionism are neurotic regressions to earlier stages of sexual development.[24] With much less animus against these alleged neuroses and with a much more sympathetic attitude towards sports, Daniel Dervin has written in a recent article published in *The Psychoanalytic Review* that "the perfect self is on exhibition [in athletics] as in no other comparable performance. The athlete's goal of winning comprises a narcissistic triumph, accompanied by restored self-esteem and elation. . . ."[25]

Body builders are surely the extreme case. When they compete, comments one scholar rather feverishly, "whole anatomies are pumped like priapic erections, contracting poses and shifting with held violence from one pose to the next with the vaginal contractions of labor pains."[26] This comment seems almost as exhibitionistic as the body builders it satirizes. Still, the mirror-mirror-on-the-wall atmosphere of Gold's Gym does suggest at least a touch of narcissism.

Given the pejorative connotations of the terms in most psychoanalytic literature and in ordinary speech, not many people want to admit that they are narcissists or exhibitionists, but how else can we explain the craze for physical fitness, which holds millions in its spell, if these millions do not want to inhabit bodies which are, if not perfect, at least more nearly perfect than they were before the exercises began? "Fame is the spur," wrote John Milton, "that last infirmity of noble mind." Perhaps vanity is the spur for those of us without noble minds. What else, if not vanity, if not a harmless form of narcissism, can explain the efforts we make to remain youthful and—let us admit it—to be as sexually attractive as possible? To what else do the advertisers appeal when they show us the beautiful bodies of young men and women who use the right equipment, run in the right shoes, and stick to the right diet?

If one admits that narcissism and exhibitionism are frequent motives for sports participation, one must still face the most difficult question of all: do athletes experience their athletic performances as erotic? Literary examples suggest to me that they might—at least in those sports where the pattern of movement is similar to that in unquestionably erotic situations. Consider an episode from Plato's *Symposium*. The appropriateness of the source is suggested by Freud's comment, in the preface to the fourth edition of *Three Essays* (1920), that "the *eros* of the divine Plato" approached "the extended sexuality of psychoanalysis."[27] In the episode, Alcibiades complains to the group that his ardent love for Socrates is unrequited:

Well, he and I were alone together, and I thought that when there was nobody with us, I should hear him speak the language which lovers use to their loves when they are by themselves, and I was delighted. Nothing of the sort; he conversed as usual, and spent the day with me, and then went away. Afterwards I challenged him to the palaestra; and he wrestled and closed with me several times when there was no one present; I fancied that I might succeed in this manner. Not a bit; I made no way with him.[28]

One might object that Alcibiades' motives are purely erotic and not athletic at all, but that is not the point. He expected Socrates to be as sexually aroused by their grapple as he was.

The novels and essays of Norman Mailer provide a plethora of instances of the intersection of sport and eros, most notably in his story, "The Time of Her Time," but the best literary example is probably the famous scene in chapter 20 of D. H. Lawrence's novel, *Women in Love* (1921), where Gerald and Birkin wrestle:

So the two men entwined and wrestled with each other, working nearer and nearer. Both were white and clear, but Gerald flushed smart red where he was touched, and Birkin remained white and tense. He seemed to penetrate into Gerald's more solid, more diffuse bulk, to interfuse his body through the body of the other, as if to bring it subtly into subjection, always seizing with some rapid necromantic foreknowledge every motion of the other flesh. . . . It was as if Birkin's whole physical intelligence interpentrated into Gerald's body, as if his fine sublimated energy entered into the flesh of the fuller man, like some potency, casting a fine net, a prison, through the muscles into the very depths of Gerald's physical being.

Ann Hall has discussed this passage and asserted that "the Lawrentian wrestle has no relevance for women,"[29] but her ability to imagine female equivalence is probably hampered by conventional assumptions about sexual roles. The recent film, *Personal Best*, includes a steamy scene in which two female athletes arm wrestle and then make love.

These examples might be dismissed as eccentric, but Freud, once again, can be cited: "The fact is," he wrote, "that a number of persons have reported that they experienced the first signs of genital arousal when scrapping or wrestling with their playmates. Effective in such situations is not only general muscular exertion but also ample skin-contact with one's opponent."[30] It seems to me that the experiences dramatized by Lawrence in *Women in Love* and by Robert Towne in

Personal Best can be understood as extrapolations of the impulse that brings two boxers to embrace at the end of a hideously punitive match.

The psychic force of attraction between athletic opponents is often—perhaps usually—overwhelmed by the contrary, hostile forces of antagonism, but the aggressiveness unleashed in team sports is commonly accompanied by an intense emotional bond among teammates. Once again, a literary example captures the essence of the phenomenon. In Mark Harris's *Bang the Drum Slowly*, the narrator, a pitcher named Henry Wiggen, says this about his teammates:

> You felt warm towards them, and you looked at them, and them at you, and you were both alive, and you might as well said, "Ain't it something? Being alive, I mean! Ain't it really quite a great thing at that?" and if they would of been a girl you would of kissed them, though you never said such a thing out loud but only went on about your business.[31]

Team sports not only create an intense emotional bond; they also provide a socially acceptable context for the physical expression of these otherwise repressed emotions. Who has not noticed the uninhibited acrobatic embraces of male ballplayers as they celebrate a score? Their unchallenged masculinity allows them the privilege of orgiastic gesture. At the same time, rumors of lesbianism often rob female teammates of a like opportunity to express affection.

Having cited Freud several times, having returned to the Freudian assertion that sadism and masochism are both sexual in origin, I want now to look somewhat more closely at the contributions of psychoanalysis. In a footnote added to the second edition of *Three Essays* (1910), Freud wrote, "It is well known that sports are widely used by modern educators to distract youth from sexual activity. It would be more correct to say that sports replace sexual pleasure with the pleasure of movement and push sexual activity back upon its autoerotic components."[32] Had Freud been more familiar with the English public schools of his day, he might have commented on the role played by sports in the encouragement of the homoerotic behavior that was apparently rife in such schools.

When analyzing the sources of infantile sexuality, Freud commented on "the creation of sexual excitement through rhythmical . . . shaking of the body" and on the extraordinary sensual pleasure that accompanies vigorous muscular exertion.[33] Arnold Plack extended these remarks in his book *Society and Evil*. Plack asserted the existence of an erotic component in running, leaping, throwing, riding, in almost every kind of human movement. He is especially provocative when he comments on horseback riding:

> If one doesn't want to ride one's horse to lameness, one must consciously or unconsciously move with one's back, pelvic, and thigh muscles as in sexual intercourse. . . . It needn't necessarily lead to ejaculation, but the "passionate rider" always experiences sexual relaxation.[34]

Is this why adolescent girls are notoriously fond of equestrian sports? Is this why the Lone Ranger is notoriously aloof from adolescent girls?

The psychoanalytic interpretation of sexuality and sports has not overlooked ball games. Freud implied as much in his reference to the relationship between sports and autoeroticism (quoted above). Helen Deutsch was quite explicit in her famous 1926 essay, "A Contribution to the Psychology of Sport," published in the *International Journal of Psychoanalysis*. On the basis of her work with "a patient suffering from impotence, together with anxiety-states and depression," she argued that ball games allowed the patient to overcome his phobia. Through the mastery achieved through sports, he rid himself "of part of the dread of castration or the fear of death which is common to all mankind." While this puts the emphasis on what is overcome rather than on the erotic pleasure of the act of overcoming, Deutsch did not ignore the latter, which she referred to as "the pleasurable situation of a game."[35]

If Deutsch's assertion that the soccer ball represents the genital organs of the patient's father is implausible, then total disbelief is the appropriate response to another famous essay, "Psycho-Analytic Reflections on the Development of Ball Games," by the British psychiatrist Adrian Stokes. In his farfetched analysis, Stokes imagines the lacrosse goal to be "the archetypal vagina" and comments on a rugby game as follows: "Ejected out of the mother's body, out of the scrum, after frantic hooking and pushing, there emerges the rich loot of the father's genital."[36]

Despite my deep reservations about this kind of off-the-wall psychoanalysis, I am persuaded by the argument of an essay appearing in a recent issue of the *Journal of Psychoanalytical Anthropology*. Analyzing the obscene chants of Argentine soccer fans, which are too graphically disgusting to quote, Marcelo Mario Suarez-Orozco demonstrates that the fans employ sexual metaphors to boast of their virility and to sneer at the opposition's alleged homosexuality. The soccer goal is not a symbolic vagina, as in the silly essay by Stokes, but rather a symbolic anus, which must be defended from penetration. The frenzy of the fans and the violence of their language led Suarez-Orozco to conclude that they "are attracted to the soccer field in order to find a therapeutic outlet for their taboo thoughts." Their excessive fears he interprets as "an unconscious and forbidden wish."[37]

While my positivistic impulses continue to rebel against some of the absurdities of Freud and his followers, I am absolutely convinced that the joy of sports, for both the spectator and the participant, has as much to do with eros—in *some* form—as with the disinterested aesthetic contemplation of physical skills or the sense of achievement obtained by a good play. In our own time, the erotic element in sports has once again become visible—as it was in the pagan cultures of classical antiquity. The easy acceptance of athletic eroticism in ancient Greece and Rome stands in sharp contrast to the reticence and denial that have long characterized our own responses. Why has this been so? Why have we long cherished the myth of asexual sports? I do *not* believe, as many of my neo-Marxist colleagues do, that modern hypocrisy is the result of capitalism's alleged need to repress, sublimate, and exploit the instinctual self. The difference between ancient awareness and modern denial has much more to do with the difference between paganism and Christianity than with the rise of corporate capitalism. A moment's thought should convince anyone that the emergent realization of the erotic element in sports is related to the relative weakness of late twentieth-century Christianity rather than to the demise of corporate capitalism. If corporate capitalism *were* the explanation for the denial of eros, we should now feel the taboo more intensely than ever.

Let me conclude then with three minimal assertions:

(1) The spectator's admiration for athletes and their performances is to some degree tinged if not positively steeped in erotic impulses;

(2) The pleasure that athletes experience in their performances may have roots in these same mysterious impulses;

(3) It is better to investigate and test these possibilities than prudishly to deny them.

Recall Plato's *Symposium*, which encouraged Freud in his speculations about libido. Alcibiades was, as William Butler Yeats noted, a great rogue, but he was a lot more sophisticated about sexuality than those who still believe the myth that there is no relationship whatsoever between sport and eros.

NOTES

For their suggestions I wish to thank Steven L. Ablon, John A. Cameron, Donald G. Kyle, and Andrew Parker.

1. Christine Kulke, "Emanzipation oder gleiches Recht auf 'Trimm Dich'?" *Sport in der Klassengesellschaft*, ed. Gerhard Vinnai (Munich: Fischer, 1972), 101.

2. Sigmund Freud, *Werkausgabe: Drei Abhandlungen zur Sexualtheorie*, ed. Anna Freud and Ilse Grubrich-Simitis, 2 vols. (Frankfurt: Fischer, 1978), 1: 249.

3. On play and display, see Gregory P. Stone's often reprinted article, "American Sports: Play and Display," *Chicago Review* 9 (1955): 83–100.

4. K. J. Dover, "Classical Greek Attitudes to Sexual Behaviour," *Women in the Ancient World*, ed. John Peradotto and J. P. Sullivan (Albany: State University of New York Press, 1984), 152; see also K. J. Dover, *Greek Homosexuality* (Cambridge: Harvard University Press, 1978).

5. Edgar Z. Friedenberg, "The Changing Role of Homoerotic Fantasy in Spectator Sports," *Jock*, ed. Donald F. Sabo, Jr., and Ross Runfola (Englewood Cliffs: Prentice-Hall, 1980), 179–80.

6. Brian Stoddart, *Saturday Afternoon Fever* (North Ryde, N.S.W.: Angus and Robertson, 1986), 150.

7. See Sigrid Paul, "The Wrestling Tradition and Its Social Functions," *Sport in Africa*, ed. William J. Baker and J. A. Mangan (New York: Africana Publishing Co., 1987), 24, 30–31.

8. Carl Diem, *Weltgeschichte des Sports*, 3rd ed., 2 vols. (Frankfurt: Cotta Verlag, 1971), 1: 14.

9. See Alyce Taylor Cheska, "Ball Games Played by North American Indian Women," *The History, the Evolution and Diffusion of Sports and Games in Different Cultures*, ed. Roland Renson et al. (Brussels: Bestuur voor de Lichamelijke Opvoeding, de Sport en het Openluchtleven, 1976), 39–56; Alyce Taylor Cheska, "Ball Game Participation of North American Indian Women," *Her Story in Sport*, ed. Reet Howell (West Point: Leisure Press, 1982), 19–34.

10. See Lilly Kahil, "Mythological Repertoire of Brauron," *Ancient Greek Art and Iconography*, ed. Warren G. Moon (Madison: University of Wisconsin Press, 1983), 231–44; Lilly Kahil, "L'Artémis de Brauron: Rites et Mystère," *Antike Kunst* 20 (1977): 86–98; Erika Simon, *Festivals of Attica* (Madison: University of Wisconsin Press, 1983), 83–88; Thomas F. Scanlon, "The Footrace of the Heraia at Olympia," *Ancient World* 8 (1984): 77–90; Thomas F. Scanlon, "Virgineum Gymnasium: Spartan Females and Early Greek Athletics," in Wendy J. Raschke, ed., *The Archaeology of the Olympics* (Madison: University of Wisconsin Press, 1988), 185–216.

11. Xenophon, *Constitution of the Spartans* [1.4], trans. H. G. Daykins, *The Greek Historians*, ed. F. R. B. Godolphin, 2 vols. (New York: Random House, 1942), II: 658–59.

12. Giampiera Arrigoni, "Donne e Sport nel Mundo Greco," *Le Donne in Grecia*, ed. Giampiera Arrigoni (Bari: Editori Laterza, 1985), 66.

13. Propertius, *The Poems of Propertius* [3.14], trans. John Warden (Indianapolis: Bobbs-Merrill, 1972), 166–67.

14. Juvenal, *Satires*, trans. Rolfe Humphries (Bloomington: Indiana University Press, 1958), Satire 6, p. 67.

15. Michael Grant, *The Gladiators* (London: Weidenfeld and Nicolson, 1967), 37.

16. See Norbert Elias, *Ueber den Prozess der Zivilisation*, rev. ed., (Frankfurt: Suhrkamp, 1976); Norbert Elias and Eric Dunning, *Quest for Excitement: Sport and Leisure in the Civilizing Process* (Oxford: Basil Blackwell, 1986).

17. On the civilizing of the medieval tournament, see Allen Guttmann, *Sports Spectators* (New York: Columbia University Press, 1986), 35–46.

18. Werner Koerbs, *Vom Sinn der Leibesuebungen zur Zeit der italienischen Renaissance*, ed. Wolfgang Decker (1938; reprint ed. Hildesheim: Weidmann, 1988), 17–18; Martine Boiteux, "Chasse aux Taureaux et Jeux Romains de la Renaissance," *Les Jeux de la Renaissance*, ed. Philippe Ariès and Jean-Claude Margolin (Paris: Vrin, 1982), 39; Klaus Zieschang, *Vom Schuetzenfest zum Turnfest* (Ahrensburg: Czwalina, 1977), 82–83; F. K. Mathys, *Spiel und Sport im alten Basel* (Basel: Cratander, 1954), 19; Walter Schaufelberger, *Der Wettkampf in der alten Eidgenossenschaft* (Basel: Paul Haupt, 1972), 90.

19. Quoted in Janice Kaplan, *Women and Sports* (New York: Viking Press, 1979), 77.

20. Linda Huey, *A Running Start: An Athlete, a Woman* (New York: Quadrangle Books, 1976), 204, 209.

21. Tony Duffy and Paul Wade, *Winning Women* (New York: TIME Books, 1983), 9.

22. Sigmund Freud, "Triebe und Triebschicksale" (1915), in *Werkausgabe* (see note 2, above), 1: 267–85.

23. Kenneth Clark, *The Nude* (New York: Pantheon Books, 1956), 8.

24. Ulrich Dix, *Sport und Sexualitaet* (Frankfurt: Maerz Verlag, 1972).

25. Daniel Dervin, "A Psychoanalysis of Sports," *The Psychoanalytic Review* 72 (Summer 1985) 2: 288.

26. Alphonso Lingis, "Orchids and Muscles," *Philosophic Inquiry in Sport*, ed. William J. Morgan and Klaus V. Meier (Champaign: Human Kinetics, 1988), 125.

27. Freud, *Drei Abhandlungen*, *Werkausgabe* (see note 2, above), 1: 238.

28. Plato, *Symposium*, 217c (Jowett translation).

29. M. Ann Hall, "Women and the Lawrentian Wrestle," *Arena Review* 3 (May, 1979) 2: 25.

30. Freud, *Drei Abhandlungen*, *Werkausgabe* (see note 2, above), 1: 288–89.

31. Mark Harris, *Bang the Drum Slowly* (1956; reprint ed. New York: Anchor Books, 1962), 196–97.

32. Freud, *Drei Abhandlungen*, *Werkausgabe* (see note 2, above), 1: 289n.

33. Ibid., 1: 287.

34. Arnold Plack, *Die Gesellschaft und das Boese* (Munich: List Verlag, 1969), 224.

35. Helen Deutsch, "A Contribution to the Psychology of Sport," *International Journal of Psychoanalysis* 7 (1926): 225–27.

36. Adrian Stokes, "Psycho-Analytic Reflections on the Development of Ball

Games," *Sport and Society,* ed. Alex Natan (London: Bowes and Bowes, 1958), 175. Originally published in the *International Journal of Psychoanalysis* in 1955.

37. Marcelo Mario Suarez-Orozco, "A Study of Argentine Soccer," *Journal of Psychoanalytic Anthropology* 5 (Winter 1982) 1: 23–24. See also Alan Dundes, "Into the Endzone for a Touchdown: A Psychoanalytic Interpretation of American Football," *Western Folklore* 37 (1978): 75–88.

Essays on Sport History and Sport Mythology was composed into type on a Linotron 202 digital phototypesetter in ten point Caledonia with three points of spacing between the lines. Caledonia was also selected for display. The book was typeset by G&S Typesetters, Inc., printed offset by Thomson-Shore, Inc., and bound by John H. Dekker & Sons, Inc. The paper on which this book is printed carries acid-free characteristics for an effective life of at least three hundred years.

TEXAS A&M UNIVERSITY PRESS: COLLEGE STATION